WHAT EVERY FOOTBALL FAN SHOULD KNOW

Football Facts & Rules
Skills, Positions, Tactics & Matchday Culture

by

Theo Curio

What Every Young Football Fan Should Know

Football facts, skills & rules explained — a guide to positions, tactics & matchday culture

TABLE OF CONTENTS

INTRODUCTION

Hey, football friend!

Think of this book as your sidekick for watching and talking about the game. Inside, you'll get simple explainers of the **Laws**, clear maps of **positions** and **formations**, kid-ready tips on **tactics**, plus fun facts and trivia for **matchday**.

This isn't a training plan. It's **explained, not coached**: what the lines mean, why a flag goes up, how **offside** works, and what the referee's signals tell you.

Football is for **everyone** — girls, boys, all ages and backgrounds. Please **play kindly**, respect the officials, and follow your coach and **parents or guardians** for safety. If the **Laws** change after printing, the best habit still wins: **look carefully, think clearly, play fairly**.

Ready? Kick off!

CHAPTER 1

FROM ANCIENT GAMES TO MODERN FOOTBALL

Football didn't appear overnight. It grew from older ball games played in streets, courts, and temple yards. The same ideas kept returning: **control a ball, protect it**, and **aim for a target**. Over centuries, people moved from wild scrambles to shared rules and marked pitches. Step by step, a rough crowd chase became the organised, fast game you watch today.

1.1 ANCIENT BALL GAMES

Centuries before modern football, people across the world were already kicking, guiding, and aiming the ball. In China, **cuju** used a stitched leather ball and a small net; outfield players didn't use their hands, so control and accuracy mattered more than force. In Japan, **kemari** was a calm keep-up circle: teammates passed the ball with their feet and bodies to keep it in the air for as long as possible.

Around the Mediterranean, Greeks and Romans played tougher team games such as **episkyros** and **harpastum**. Teams tried to carry or move a ball past a line or into a space while blocking opponents. Hands were often allowed, so the play felt rougher than

today's football. still it taught shielding, teamwork, and territory—ideas you can recognise on any pitch now.

Far away in the Americas, players on a long stone court used their hips, thighs, and shoulders to strike a heavy rubber ball, sometimes aiming through a high ring. This **Mesoamerican** game demanded timing, strength, and precise body control. Different rules, different skills—but the same heartbeat: **keep the ball under control** and **reach a target** while a crowd watches and cares.

1.2 MEDIEVAL "MOB FOOTBALL"

Street Chaos

Before tidy pitches and shared laws, whole towns chased one ball through streets and fields. Hundreds of people joined in, pushing and scrambling toward far-apart goals—sometimes a bridge, a gate, or a tree. Team sizes weren't fixed. The route wasn't fixed. The rules? Almost none. It was noisy, rough, and exciting, but not very safe for players, shops, windows, or anyone in the way.

Push for Order

As towns grew, this chaos clashed with everyday life. Crowds blocked roads, damaged property, and caused injuries. Leaders tried to control or ban the games on busy days. Players still loved the thrill, but many wanted something

fairer: **set spaces to play, clear limits on contact,** and **the same rules wherever teams met**. That push for order led schools and clubs to write down codes, agree on team sizes, and mark out proper pitches. Bit by bit, the wild crowd chase shrank into a balanced match that two elevens could actually finish—and enjoy.

1.3 SCHOOL & CLUB CODES

Different Rulebooks

Schools and towns ran **their own versions** of football. Some let players **carry or pick up** the ball; others banned hands for everyone but a keeper. One code used a **strict offside** (few forward passes), while another had **no offside** at all. Restarts varied—**kick-ins** from the touchline in some places, **throw-ins** in others. Even **team sizes**, **goal sizes**, and what counted as **fair contact** (tripping, "hacking" at shins) could change from town to town. Friendly matches often stalled because teams **couldn't agree on which rulebook to use.**

Early Written Codes

To fix that, groups at **Cambridge** and in **Sheffield** drew up **clear written rules** so mixed teams could actually play. They listed what happens after the ball goes out (**who restarts and how**), which fouls earn a **free kick**, and how a **goal is scored**. Many codes also **banned tripping and hacking**, set basic **pitch markings**, and tried to define **handling** and **offside** in plain terms. The lists weren't identical, but they made matches **playable**: both sides agreed **before kick-off**.

Towards One Game

As clubs travelled more, the need for **one shared set of laws** became obvious. Committees compared the local codes, kept the **simple, repeatable ideas**, and dropped confusing ones. Common elements settled in: **marked rectangles, fixed team sizes** (eleven a side), **standard restarts** (throw-in, goal kick, corner), and **free kicks** for certain fouls. With a **common language** for play, teams from different towns could meet, finish a match, and know the result was **fair**.

1.4 1863 & THE FA

Club and school teams wanted matches that didn't stall over rule arguments, so representatives met in **London in 1863** to agree on a single code. They formed **The Football Association (FA)** and set out to publish one list of laws that any two teams could use.

No Hacking, No Carrying

The sharpest fight was over **handling and hacking**. Some clubs liked carrying the ball and kicking at opponents' shins. The FA side **banned carrying** (for outfielders) and **outlawed hacking and tripping**, aiming for a feet-first, safer game. A few clubs walked out, and the rugby style continued on its own path—**association football** and rugby football **split**.

From First Laws to a Shared Game

The first FA laws fixed **basic restarts** and tidied up fouls. **Offside** was very strict at first—anyone ahead of the ball risked a whistle—but within a few years it was **relaxed** so forward passing could grow. Bit by bit, common **pitch markings**, throw-ins, goal kicks, and corners made games **repeatable** and results **fair** wherever teams met.

FACT: "Association football" was shortened to "assoc.", then nicknamed "soccer"—a word that began in Britain.

1.5 KEY LAWS TIMELINE

After the FA chose **one code** in 1863, the laws didn't freeze. They were **tuned step by step** to make matches clearer, fairer, and faster. Here are the big steps you'll still notice today.

1863: ONE CODE

Shared laws replace local rulebooks. Handling (for outfielders) and hacking are banned.

1866: OFFSIDE LOOSENED

No longer "anyone ahead of the ball." Attackers need opponents between them and the goal before a flag—more forward passing.

1872: CORNER KICK

A standard restart from the corner flag. Teams can plan set-piece routines.

1891: PENALTY & GOAL NETS

The **penalty kick** arrives for serious fouls near the goal. **Nets** show clearly when the ball is in.

1902: THE BOXES & SPOT

The **penalty area, goal area**, and **penalty spot** are marked. Decisions get quicker and fairer.

1925: 2-DEFENDER OFFSIDE

You're onside if **two defenders** (often a defender + keeper) are nearer the goal line than you. More goals, quicker play.

1960S: SUBSTITUTES

Injured players can be replaced; later, tactical subs change late-game plans.

1970: YELLOW & RED CARDS

Visible cards make discipline clear to players and fans.

1992: BACK-PASS RULE

Keepers can't handle a deliberate pass from a teammate's foot. Time-wasting drops; defenders must play.

2010S: GOAL-LINE TECH

Electronics confirm if the **whole ball** crossed the line. Referees get instant signals.

2018-NOW: VAR

Video checks goals, penalties, reds, and mistaken identity. Calibrated lines (and newer tracking) help with tight offsides.

1.6 THE GLOBAL GAME & WOMEN'S FOOTBALL

Once teams shared the same laws, football **travelled fast**. Sailors, students and workers carried it to **Europe, Africa, Asia and the Americas**. Railways and newspapers helped clubs set fixtures. Because everyone now used **one code**, strangers could meet, play, and trust the result.

Organising the World

As cross-border matches grew, countries formed **national associations**, and a world body organised **international tournaments**. Referees learned the same signals, pitches used the **same markings**, and youth events taught the next generation. The heart stays simple: **11 v 11, one ball, one goal at a time**. As the game spread to more places, it also spread to **more people**—which raised a vital question: **who gets to play?**

Women's Football: Early Crowds, Setbacks, Big Return

BRITISH LADES' FOOTBALL CLUB
FIRST OFFICIAL MATCK
ENGLAND 1895

Women and girls formed teams early and drew **large crowds** in the 1900s. Then came **bans and limits** in many countries, slowing progress for years. Those bans were lifted. Investment returned. Today, girls and women play from **grassroots to elite level**, with **record attendances**, professional leagues in many nations, and national teams competing at major tournaments.

1.7 TWENTY DATES EVERY FAN SHOULD KNOW

Moments that changed the game

With one code agreed upon and the sport spreading to more people, certain decisions and firsts shaped the football you watch today. Here's a quick, kid-friendly map.

1863 — The Football Association forms in London; one shared code replaces local rulebooks (no carrying, no hacking).

1866 — **Offside** is relaxed so forward passing can grow.

1871–72 — The first national **cup** competition is played.

1872 — The first official **international** match takes place.

1872 — The **corner kick** becomes a standard restart.

1888 — The first organised **league** launches a home-and-away season.

1891 — The **penalty kick** is introduced; **goal nets help confirm when the ball is in**

1902 — The **penalty area, goal area**, and **penalty spot** are marked on the pitch.

1904 — A world body forms to organise **international football**.

1921 — A major ban restricts **women's football** in parts of the UK (later lifted).

1925 — **Offside** changes to the "**two defenders**" rule— more goals, faster play.

1930 — The first **World Cup** is held.

1965 — **Substitutions** arrive in league matches (first for injuries, then tactics).

1970 — **Yellow and red cards** make discipline clear to players and fans.

1971 — The UK ban on **women's football** is lifted; the game begins to rebuild.

1991 — The first **Women's World Cup** crowns a world champion.

1992 — The **back-pass rule** stops keepers from handling a teammate's pass from the foot.

1992 — England's top division becomes the modern **Premier League.**

2012 — **Goal-line technology** is approved to confirm whether the whole ball crossed the line.

2018 — **VAR** begins at major tournaments to check goals, penalties, and red cards.

CHAPTER 2
THE MATCH AT A GLANCE

A football match is a tidy contest with simple rhythms: a start, a flow, stoppages, and a finish. Two elevens face off on a marked pitch, the referee keeps time, and the score decides everything. Learn these beats, and the rest of the game—rules, positions, tactics—will make instant sense.

2.1 WHAT IS A MATCH?

A match follows a clear rhythm: kick-off, flowing play, stoppages, and a finish. Know these beats, and every decision makes quick sense.

Kick-Off & Ends

A **coin toss** sets who starts and which way teams attack. Play begins with a **kick-off** from the centre spot. **Teams swap** ends at half-time.

Time & Score

The standard length is **two halves of 45 minutes**. The referee keeps the watch. Goals change the **scoreline**; the team with more at full-time **wins**.

Added Time

Injuries, substitutions, and delays don't shorten the game. The referee adds **stoppage time** at the end of each half to make up for lost minutes

Draws vs Knockouts

In **league** play, a level score is a **draw**, and both teams get a point. In **cup** ties, a draw may lead to **extra time** (two 15-minute halves) and then a **penalty shootout** to find a winner.

Substitutions

Teams bring a bench of players and can use a **set number of subs** (the exact number depends on the competition). A sub only enters with the referee's permission, at a **stoppage**.

Restarts You'll See

After the ball goes out or a foul is given, play restarts with a **throw-in, goal kick, corner, free kick, drop ball**, or **penalty**—each has its own simple steps you'll learn next.

2.2 PITCH & MARKINGS

Those white lines aren't decoration—they're the game's **secret instructions**. Learn them, and you'll start reading decisions **before** the whistle.

Lines & Boundaries — The border that decides everything

The pitch is a rectangle with **touchlines** (long sides) and **goal lines** (short sides). A line **belongs to the area it marks**: the ball is out only when the **whole ball** fully crosses it. Because the ball is round, even a thin slice still touching the line keeps play in. Assistant referees watch these edges to judge whether the ball is out of play and whether a goal has been scored.

Halfway Line & Centre Circle — Space for a fair start

The **halfway line** splits the field; the **centre spot** starts each half and restarts after goals. The **centre circle** keeps opponents **9.15 metres** away so the first pass isn't crushed instantly. The kick-off may go **backwards or forwards**; once the ball moves, anyone can challenge.

Penalty Area & Spot — Where small mistakes become big chances

The big rectangle is the **penalty area: 16.5 metres** from the goal line and **16.5 metres** from each post. Direct free kick offences by the defending team here result in a penalty (11 metres). The **goalkeeper may handle** the ball **inside** this area; outside it, keepers are outfield players.

Goal Area — The keeper's launch pad

The smaller rectangle is the **goal area** (about **5.5 metres** from each post and into the field). **Goal kicks** and defending free kicks inside this space are taken **from anywhere in it**. Since the 2019 law change, the ball is **in play when it's kicked and clearly moves**, so short, quick restarts are common.

Penalty Arc — A safety bubble at penalties

The arc at the box edge isn't part of the area. It simply marks **9.15 metres** from the **penalty spot**, keeping all players (except the taker and the keeper) back until the kick is taken. The moment the ball moves, teammates may **enter the box**.

Corner Arcs & Flags — Tiny arcs, big chances

Each corner has a **1-metre** arc and a **fixed flag**. For a corner kick, the ball must **touch or sit inside** the arc; the flag stays upright. Attackers often use quick corners; defenders must give the taker **9.15 metres** of space until the ball is in play.

Goals & Nets — What truly makes a goal

A goal counts only when the **whole ball** crosses the **goal line**, **between the posts** and **under the bar**. Nets help everyone see, but the **line** decides. Where used, **goal-line technology** tells the referee if the ball has fully crossed.

Sizes & Surfaces — Same language on any pitch

Pitch sizes can vary within set limits; **youth pitches** are smaller, but the **markings mean the same things**. Surfaces may be natural grass or approved **3G/4G** turf; markings must be **clear and consistent** whatever the field.

2.3 BALL, KiT & ARMBAND

Before a single pass, the **ball** decides how the match feels, the **kit** keeps players safe and easy to tell apart, and one **armband** says who speaks for the team.

The Ball — feel, size, pressure

Match balls are built to fly true and bounce fairly. Adult games use a **size 5** (about **68–70 cm** around, **410–450 g**), while most young players use **size 4**; younger players still use **size 3**. The ball is pumped to the right pressure so it's neither a rock nor a sponge—competitions check this before kick-off. Surfaces vary (grass, 3G/4G), but the markings and decisions don't: the **whole ball** must cross a line to be out or to count as a goal.

Boots & Safety — studs and shinpads

Players wear boots suited to the surface: **moulded studs** or blades for firm ground, longer studs for soft ground, and turf soles for artificial pitches. **Shin pads are compulsory** and must be covered by socks. Anything dangerous— **jewellery, sharp studs, loose accessories**—is not  allowed. Referees can stop play until a player is safe to continue.

Kit Colours & Numbers — who's who at a glance

Two teams must wear **clearly different colours** so passes and decisions stay clean. **Goalkeepers wear colours that stand out** from both teams and the match officials. Shirts carry **numbers** so everyone can tell who did what. If players wear undershirts or leggings, they should **match the main kit colour** to avoid confusion.

The Captain's Armband — the team's voice

One player wears a **captain's armband**. Captains join the **coin toss**, help calm teammates, and **speak to the referee respectfully** when clarification is needed. They don't gain extra powers in the laws—but their **voice and example** shape the team's behaviour.

2.4 WHO'S IN CHARGE?

The whistle and the flags are there to keep the match safe, fair, and flowing. Know who does what, and every decision makes sense.

The Referee — final say, fair play

The referee keeps time, starts and restarts play, and applies the **Laws of the Game**. They manage **fouls and free kicks**, play **advantage** when it helps the attacking team, and give **yellow** or **red cards** when needed. Before kick-off, they check **balls, goals, and player safety** (no jewellery, shin pads on), then hold the **coin toss** with both captains.

The referee can **change a decision** on the advice from other officials—but **only before play restarts**. Their job is not to be popular; it's to keep the game **fair**.

Assistant Referees — eyes on lines and offside

Two assistant referees (ARs) patrol the touchlines. They **judge** when the ball is out of play and show which team's **throw-in** it is with the flag. Most importantly, they track the **second-last defender** to help with **offside**. They can also signal **fouls** near them and **corner** and goal-kick decisions. Clear signals help everyone understand the next restart.

Fourth Official — the organiser on the sideline

At higher levels, the fourth official manages **substitutions**, checks players' equipment, and keeps the **technical areas** calm. They lift the board for **added time** and confirm changes with the referee. If an assistant can't continue, the fourth official can **step in**.

Video Match Officials (where used) — quiet checks

Some competitions use **video assistant (VAR)** to help with **four** big things: **goals, penalties, direct red cards**, and **mistaken identity**. Reviews focus on **clear and obvious** errors. The referee may do an **on-field review** on a pitch-side screen, but the **final decision** still belongs to the referee.

Coaches & Captains — influence, not authority

Coaches may instruct from the technical area but must behave; they never run onto the pitch without permission. The **captain's armband** doesn't add legal power, but captains can **speak respectfully** to the referee and help calm teammates.

Youth Matches — fewer officials, same laws

Many youth games have only a referee (and sometimes volunteer club assistants). **The laws are the same**; signals and safety checks still apply, just with fewer people to run them.

> <u>**FACT:**</u> **VAR can only review goals, penalties, direct red cards, and cases of mistaken identity — not throw-ins, corners, or routine free kicks.**

2.5 SCORELINES & TABLES

Numbers tell the story. The **scoreline** shows who won today; the **table** shows who's winning the season.

Scorelines — Reading the result

Results are written as two numbers: **home – away**. 2–1 means the home team scored two and the away team one; 0–0 is **nil–nil**. In some knockout rounds, the two legs are added together on **aggregate** to decide the winner

Points — How wins become league positions

Most leagues award **3 points for a win, 1 for a draw, and 0 for a loss.** Over months, points stack up. A single win can

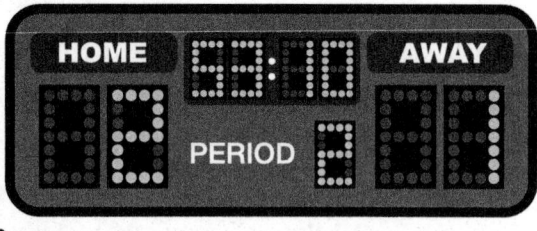

jump a team several places if rivals draw or lose.

The Table — Columns that matter

Tables usually show **P** (played), **W** (wins), **D** (draws), **L** (losses), **GF** (goals for), **GA** (goals against), **GD** (goal difference), and **Pts** (points). **GD = GF - GA.** Teams are ranked mainly by **Pts**.

Goal Difference — Why margins matter

When teams have the **same points**, most competitions use **goal difference** first. A team that wins 3–0 and loses 0–1 has GD of **+2**—better than two 1–0 wins and a 0–2 loss (**+0**).

Tiebreakers — When points are level

After GD, many leagues use **goals scored** next. Some use **head-to-head** records (results between the tied teams), and a few use **fair play** or a **playoff** if everything is still equal. The competition rules decide the order.

Form & Fixtures — The road ahead

A form line (like **W W D L W**) shows recent results. **Games in hand** mean a team has **played fewer matches**—use **P** to check. The **run-in** (the final fixtures) often decides champions, European places, and relegation escapes.

2.6 COMMON RESTARTS

Restarts are tiny reset buttons. Learn them, and you'll predict the next pass before the ball is live.

Kick-Off — the first touch

Starts each half and after goals. The ball is on the **centre spot**, and opponents are outside the **centre circle**. The ball is in play when it's **kicked and clearly moves**—it may go **backwards or forwards**.

Throw-In — from the touchline

Given when the ball fully crosses a **touchline**. The taker faces the field, throws with **both hands from behind and over the head**, with **both feet on or behind** the line. You can't **score directly** from a throw-in; a bad technique results in a throw-in to the other team.

Goal Kick — building from the back

Awarded when attackers last touch the ball over the **goal line** (not a goal). Taken from **anywhere in the goal area**. Since 2019, the ball is in play when it's **kicked and moves; opponents must stay outside the penalty area** until then. You're **not offside** from a goal kick.

Corner Kick — a set-piece chance

Given when defenders last touch the ball over their **goal line** (not a goal). The ball must touch or be placed inside the corner arc; the flag stays in place; flag stays put. Opponents must give **9.15 metres**. You **can score directly** from a corner (an Olympico). No offside **directly** from the kick.

Free Kicks — direct vs indirect

A direct free kick can go straight into the goal. An indirect free kick must touch another player first (referee raises an arm until it's touched). Opponents retreat 9.15 metres; quick free kicks are allowed. If a defensive wall of three or more forms, attackers must stay 1 metre away from it.

Penalty Kick — one shot, big pressure

Awarded for certain fouls by defenders inside their penalty area. Ball on the spot (11 metres). Only the taker and keeper remain in the area;others must stay outside the box and arc. The keeper keeps at least one foot on or above the line until the kick is taken.

Dropped Ball — fair restart after a stop

Used when play stops for reasons not in the laws (e.g., injury when no foul, outside interference). Dropped to one player of the team that last touched it (or to the keeper if in the penalty area); others stand 4 metres away. A goal can't be scored directly—the ball must touch two players first.

CHAPTER 3
LAWS OF THE GAME, SIMPLY EXPLAINED

The Laws are football's **cheat codes**. Learn them and you'll hear a whistle **before** it blows, spot a foul **as** it happens, and know the restart **without** waiting for the graphics.

3.1 BALL IN/OUT OF PLAY

It isn't out just because it **looks** out. Only the **whole ball** decides everything.

Lines belong to their areas

Touchlines and goal lines are part of the field. The ball is out **only** when the **whole ball** crosses a line.—on the ground or in the air. A sliver still touching the line means play continues.

When the ball is out

- It has fully crossed a **touchline** → **throw-in**.

- It has fully crossed a **goal line** without a goal being scored → **goal kick** or **corner**.

- The referee **stops play** (injury, outside interference, serious foul).

> FACT: A ball that hits the corner flag and stays on the field is still in play.

When the ball is still in

Rebounds off the **post, bar**, a **player**, or the **referee** keep the ball in play. If the ball hits the referee and **possession changes, a promising attack starts**, or the ball **goes directly into the goal**, the referee stops play and restarts with a **dropped ball**.

Kicked and clearly moves

For **kick-offs, free kicks, corners**, and **goal kicks**, the ball is in play the moment it's **kicked and clearly moves**—not when someone just taps it and it barely wiggles.

3.2 FOULS VS FAIR CONTACT

Football allows **fair contact**, not fighting. The difference is simple: **play the ball, not the player**.

Fair Contact — shoulder, not a shove

Two players can make **shoulder-to-shoulder** contact if the ball is **within playing distance** and both try to play it. Arms must stay **tucked, no pushing** with the hands or elbows. **Shielding** is allowed—use your body to protect the ball—*only* if the ball is close enough to touch.

When it becomes a foul

If a challenge is careless (showing no regard for safety), reckless (ignoring the risk), or uses excessive force (dangerous speed or studs), it results in a **direct free kick** to the opposing team — and a **penalty** if it occurs in the defending team's **penalty area**. Common fouls include: kicking, tripping,  jumping at, charging, striking, pushing, holding, spitting, or tackling an opponent before playing the ball.

Dangerous play & impeding

A high boot near someone's head, or challenging for a ball on the ground where others could be kicked, can constitute playing in a dangerous manner — usually an indirect free kick if there's no contact. Impeding means blocking an opponent's progress without contact (indirect free kick). If you hold or bump while blocking, it becomes a direct free kick (or a penalty in the penalty area).

Cards — when discipline steps in

A reckless foul often earns a **yellow card**. Using excessive force or endangering an opponent's safety (e.g., studs-up into the ankle; serious foul play) is a **red-card offence**. Stopping an obvious goal-scoring opportunity or committing violent conduct can also result in a red card.

Quick calls you'll see:

- **Tripping from behind** when the attacker is through on goal → **direct free kick** or **penalty**; likely **yellow** (or **red** if an obvious goal-scoring opportunity).

- **Pulling a shirt** to stop a run → holding (direct free kick or penalty).

- **Hard shoulder with an elbow swing** → pushing or charging (direct free kick) and possibly a card.

- **Clean slide** that plays the ball first and only then makes light contact → play on (fair).

3.3 HANDBALL, PLAIN & SIMPLE

Handball isn't 'any ball on an arm'. It depends on what the player **does** and where the **arm** is.

The basics: what referees look for

Referees ask two quick questions: **Did** the player move the **hand** or **arm** to the ball (**deliberately**)? And is the **arm** making the body **unnaturally bigger** (stuck out **wide** or **high**)? If **yes** to either, it's usually **handball**. If the ball hits an arm from **very close range** or off the player's own body with **no time to react**, it's usually not.

FACT: For handball, the arm starts at the bottom of the armpit; the upper shoulder doesn't count as part of the arm

Usually handball

- **Moved toward the ball** (hand or arm)

- **Arm out wide** or **above shoulder**, making the body **bigger** and blocking the ball

- The **scorer's** own **accidental handball** immediately before scoring (or creating an immediate chance) is **penalised**; a **team-mate's** accidental touch earlier in the build-up is **not** a handball **offence**

Usually not handball

- Ball **deflects** from the player's **own body** onto their arm with **no time to react**

- **Arm close** to the body in a **natural position**

- A **supporting arm** used to break a **fall**, close to the body

- **Accidental handball** by a **team-mate** earlier in the build-up (**no quick score** from the arm touch)

Goalkeepers

Keepers may use their **hands inside** their own **penalty area**. **Outside** it, they're like any other player—**no handling**. A defender's handball in the box can **result in a penalty**.

Restart

Handball is a **direct free kick** to the other team or a **penalty** if the defending team commits it inside their **penalty area**.

3.4 FREE KiCKS (DiRECT & INDiRECT)

Free kicks are mini **set-pieces**. One word changes everything: **direct** or **indirect**.

Direct vs Indirect: the goal question

A **direct free kick** can be shot straight into the **goal**.

An **indirect free kick** must touch **another player** first—**team-mate** or **opponent**—before a **goal** can count. The **referee** keeps an **arm raised** to show **indirect** and **drops** it once **someone else touches the ball**.

Where & when the ball is in play

The ball must be **stationary** and the kick taken from the **correct spot**. It is **in play** when it is **kicked** and clearly **moves**. For **defensive** free kicks inside the **penalty area**, **opponents must** stay **outside the box** until the ball is **in play**.

The wall & distances

Opponents must retreat **9.15 metres**. If a **wall** of **three or more** defenders forms, **attackers must** stay **1 metre** away from it. In **older age-group** matches, the **referee** may use **vanishing spray** to mark the line.

Quick or ceremonial?

If the **fouled team** wants to go **quickly**, they usually can—**no whistle needed**—provided the ball is **still**, the **spot** is right, and no **card or lecture** is happening. If the **referee** is **setting the wall** or **showing a card, wait for the whistle** (that's a ceremonial free kick).

Common indirect situations

- **Dangerous play** with no contact (high boot near a head).

- **Impeding** without contact (blocking the path).

- **Offside**.

- **Goalkeeper offences** (e.g. holding the ball too long, handling a deliberate **back-pass**).

- **Keeper** controls the ball with **their hands** for more than **six seconds**.

- **Keeper** handles a team-mate's throw-in.

- **Restart: indirect free kick** from the place of the **offence**.

Encroachment & do-overs

If **defenders encroach** (rush the ball) before it is **in play** and **block** the kick, the **referee** may **retake** it and may **book** the encroacher. **Double-touch** by the **kicker** (taking the kick and **touching it again** before anyone else) **results in** an **indirect free kick** to the **other team**.

FACT: 9.15 metres is the same distance used for both the free-kick wall and the centre-circle radius.

3.5 PENALTIES: ONE SHOT, HUGE PRESSURE

A **penalty** turns a small mistake into the **biggest chance**. Tiny details decide things: **feet, lines**, and **encroachment**.

Set-up: spot, goalkeeper, everyone else

Ball on the **penalty spot (11 metres)**. The **kicker** is identified. The **goalkeeper** faces the ball on the **goal line**, between the **posts**. All other players wait **outside the penalty area** and the **penalty arc**, at least **9.15 metres** from the spot, until the ball **moves**. The kick must go **forward**. The ball is  in play when it is **kicked** and clearly **moves**.

Goalkeeper on the line: what's allowed

Before the kick, the **goalkeeper** may **move along the line** but not **forward off it**. At the moment of the kick, at least **one part of a foot** must be **on or above the goal line**. If the goalkeeper **steps forward early** and the kick **doesn't go in**, the kick is usually **retaken**. If the ball **does go in**, the **goal stands**.

Encroachment: stepping in too soon

Entering the **box** or **arc** before the kick is **encroachment**.

- **Attacker encroaches:**
  - **Ball in: Retake.**
  - **Ball not in: Indirect free kick to the defending team.**

- **Defender encroaches:**
  - – Ball in: Goal stands.
  - – Ball not in: Retake.
- **Both encroach: Retake.**

Feints & the second touch

Short **feints** during the **run-up** are **allowed**; a **late feint** at the moment of the kick is not—**this is unsporting behaviour.** After the kick, the **kicker** cannot **touch the ball again** until **another player** does. If it **rebounds off the goalkeeper,** the **kicker may play it.** If it comes **straight back off the post or bar,** a **second touch** by the kicker **results in** an **indirect free kick** to the **defending team.**

Common outcomes you'll recognise

- **Goalkeeper saves,** ball **spills: live play**—anyone can score.
- **Shot hits post,** returns to **kicker: indirect free kick** to the **defending team** (no **second touch**).
- **Clear early step** from the **goalkeeper,** shot **saved: retake.**
- **Attacker steps in early, scores from rebound: retake.**

3.6 OFFSIDE: KID-EASY

Offside checks where you are the **instant** a **team-mate** passes the ball. **Time your run** and you're **free.** Go **too early** and the **flag goes up.**

Position test: simple

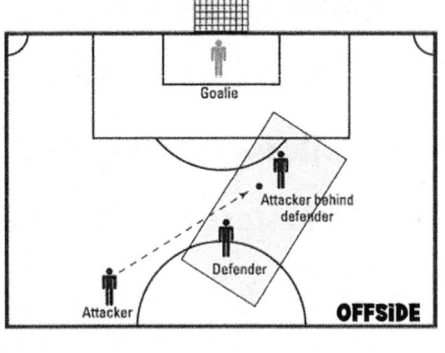

- You can only be offside in the **opponents' half**.

- You're offside if any part of your **head, body or feet** (not the **arms**) is **nearer the goal line** than both the **ball** and the **second-last opponent** at the **moment of the pass**.

- **Level** with the **second-last opponent** or the **ball is onside**.

- **Behind the ball** when it's passed **is onside**.

When it's actually an offence

Being in an **offside position** isn't a foul **in itself**. It becomes an **offence** only if, after the pass, you:

- **Play or touch** the ball.

- **Interfere with an opponent** (e.g. **block vision, challenge** for the ball, or clearly affect their ability to play).

- **Gain an advantage** from a **rebound or save** (post, bar, **goalkeeper**, or a defender's **block or clearance**).

When it's not offside

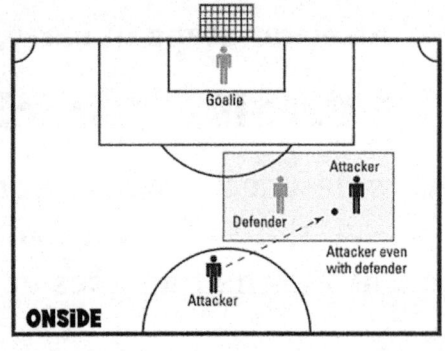

- You're in your **own half** when the pass is made.

- You're **level** with the **second-last opponent**.

- You receive the ball directly from a **goal kick, throw-in, or corner**.

- A **defender** makes a **clear**, **deliberate play** of the ball to you (not just a **deflection or save**).

Smart runs: kid-easy tips

- **Curve your run** so you **start onside**, then **attack space**.

- Look **along the line—time your move** after the passer **kicks**.

- **Defenders** beat you by **stepping up together**; one player **staying deep** breaks the **trap**.

Restarts and location

Offside means an **indirect free kick** to the **defence** from the **place** where the **offence** occurred (or where you **interfered with an opponent**).

> <u>FACT</u>: Arms don't count for offside position—refs judge by head, body, or feet.

3.7 THROW-iNS, GOAL KiCKS, CORNERS

These three **restarts** happen in almost every match. Nail the **small steps** and you'll know the decision before the **flag goes up**.

Throw-ins: from the touchline

A **throw-in is given** when the **whole ball** crosses a **touchline**. The **taker** faces the **pitch** and throws with **both hands**, from **behind and over the head**, with **both feet on or behind the line**. The ball is **in play** when it is **thrown** and **enters the pitch**. A **foul throw** (e.g. **a lifted foot, a one-handed throw, a side-arm action**) gives the **throw** to the **other team**. You **cannot score directly** from a a **throw-in**: if it goes straight into the **opponents' goal**, it's a **goal kick**; if it goes straight into **your own goal**, it's a **corner to the opponents**.

Goal kicks: building from the back

A **goal kick is given** when **attackers** last touch the ball over the **goal line** (not a goal). It is taken from **anywhere in the goal area**. The ball is **in play** when it is **kicked and clearly moves. Opponents must** stay **outside the penalty area** and **must not challenge** until the ball is **in play**; if they **enter early** and **interfere**, the **kick is retaken** (often with a **warning** or **yellow card**). Teams may **play short**; **defenders** can receive the ball inside the box once it is in play. There is no offside from a **goal kick**. You **can score directly** against the **opponents** from a **goal kick**; if it goes **directly into your own goal**, it's a **corner to the opponents**.

Corner kicks: a set-piece chance

A **corner kick is given** when **defenders** last touch the ball over **their goal line** (not a goal). The ball must be **touching or inside** the **1 metre (1 m) corner arc**, and the **corner flag** must stay **upright. Opponents retreat 9.15 metres** from the arc until the ball is **in play (is kicked and clearly moves)**. Takers can go **short** or **swing it in**—yes, you **can score directly** from a **corner (Olimpico)**. There is **no offside directly from the kick.**

> **FACT**: You cannot score directly from a throw-in; you can score directly from a corner or goal kick (against the opponents).

3.8 CARDS & DISCIPLINE

Cards keep football **safe**, **fair** and **respectful**. Yellow means a **warning**. Red means **leave the pitch**.

Yellow vs Red: what they mean

A **yellow card** is a **caution**—you **stay on** but you are **on a warning**.

A **red card** is a **sending-off**—you **leave the pitch** and your team plays with **fewer players**. **Two yellow cards** in one match **means a red card**.

When you see YELLOW (common cautions)

- **Reckless foul** (careless lunge, late trip).
- **Stopping a promising attack** (SPA) (e.g. a shirt pull to stop a break).
- **Dissent** (arguing or shouting at officials).
- **Delaying a restart** (kicking the ball away or standing over a **free kick**).
- **Not respecting the required distance** (too close at a **free kick** or **corner**—**less than 9.15 metres**).
- **Persistent fouling** (many small fouls by the same player).
- **Entering or leaving the pitch without permission.**

When you see RED (sending-off offences)

- **Serious foul play** (excessive force in a challenge for the ball; **studs** into the **ankle**).

- **Violent conduct** (hit, elbow, punch, **head-butt**—on or off the ball).

- **DOGSO** (denying an obvious goal-scoring opportunity) by a foul or by **handball** (not the **goalkeeper** in their **penalty area**).

- **Spitting** at someone.

- **Offensive, insulting** or **abusive** language or gestures.

- **Second yellow card** in the same match.

DOGSO vs SPA: kid-easy

- **DOGSO** (often **red**): last defender, attacker heading toward **goal**, close control, few or no defenders to stop them.

- **SPA (yellow)**: foul stops a **promising** move but not an obvious **goal** chance.

- **Modern change**: if **DOGSO** happens **inside the penalty area** and the defender was **clearly trying to play the ball**, it is usually a **yellow card and a penalty** (not a **red card and a penalty**). A **deliberate pull/hold** or **no attempt to play the ball** can still be **red**.

Advantage and cards

Referees can play **advantage** if the fouled team is better off, then **caution** the player at the **next stoppage**. You may see the **referee** hold up a **yellow** later and **point back** to where it happened.

Who can be carded

Players, substitutes and **team officials** (coaches) can be **cautioned** or **sent off**. If a **coach** is sent off, the team still has **11 players**. If a **player** is sent off, the team **cannot replace them**.

Restarts after cards: simple rule

- If the card comes from a **foul on the pitch**, the **restart is that free kick** (or a **penalty**).

- If the card comes from **dissent or behaviour** with **no foul**, it is an **indirect free kick** from **where it happened**.

- If **misconduct** happens when **play is stopped**, the restart **follows the original reason** for the stoppage.

Youth note

Some youth leagues use **temporary dismissals ('sin bins')** for **dissent**. That is a **local rule**—**ask your coach**. The main **Laws** use **yellow** and **red cards**.

3.9 ADVANTAGE (WHY PLAY GOES ON)

Sometimes a **foul** helps the **attacking team**, so the **referee** lets them **keep the chance**. That's **advantage**.

What it is: keep the better option

If a team is **fouled** but the ball **drops to a team-mate** in a **good position**, the **referee** can **wave play on** instead of stopping for a **free kick**. The **referee** gives it **2–3 seconds** to see if the **attack continues**.

If it **does not**, the referee **brings it back** to the **foul** and gives the **free kick** (or **penalty**).

How you'll see it

The **referee** spreads **both arms forward** and calls '**Play on, advantage!**' There is often a **delayed whistle: no whistle** if the **attack flows, a whistle** if it **stalls** within a couple of seconds.

Cards still apply

Advantage does **not** forgive the **foul**. The referee can **caution** or **send off** the player at the next **stoppage**.

- **Reckless foul results in** a **likely yellow card** later.

- **Serious foul play or violent conduct results** in a **red card** at the **next stoppage** (safety first; many **referees** stop immediately unless a clear **goal-scoring opportunity** exists).

- **DOGSO** (denying an obvious goal-scoring opportunity): if **advantage leads to a goal**, the player is usually **cautioned**; if **not**, it can still be **red**.

Where it matters most: kid-easy examples

- A **trip in midfield** but the ball **rolls to your free winger** sprinting into space—**advantage**.

- A **shove in the box** and the ball **falls to your team-mate** who **scores**—the **referee allows the goal** and **cards the defender** later.

- A **foul**, the ball **bobbles**, and your team **loses it right away**—the **referee brings it back** for the **free kick**.

When advantage is not used

- **Head injuries** or **dangerous situations: stop immediately.**

- **Offside**: once an **offside offence** occurs, **play is stopped** (no advantage to the team that **broke the law**).

- If the **foul** leaves the **attacking team** with **no realistic benefit**, the **referee stops play** straight away.

> **FACT**: A team can score after advantage is given, even for a foul inside the penalty area, and the defender can still be booked at the next stoppage.

3.10 VAR IN ONE PAGE: WHAT GETS CHECKED

Cameras help the **referee** with the **biggest decisions**—but only for **a few things**, and the **referee still decides**.

What VAR does

VAR (Video Assistant Referee) is a **video team** that watches **replays** and tells the referee if there is a **clear and obvious error** or a **serious missed incident** during a key moment. The **referee** can **keep the original decision** or **change it** after an **on-field review** at the **pitch-side monitor**.

What gets checked: only four

- **Goals**: including the short **build-up—offside, handball by the scorer,** or a **foul** just before the goal.

- **Penalties: given or not given**; also **where the foul happened** (inside or outside the **penalty area**).

- **Direct red cards: serious foul play** or **violent conduct.**

- **Mistaken identity:** the **wrong player** was shown a **card.**

How a check works: kid-easy

- After a **big event** (goal, possible **penalty** or **red card**), **VAR** does a quick **silent check.**

- If it looks **wrong,** the **referee** may do an **on-field review** (draws a **TV rectangle** with **their hands,** then watches the **monitor**).

- The **final decision** is the **referee's—not** the video room's.

What VAR does not check

Throw-ins, corners, routine **free kicks,** most **fouls in midfield,** and **second yellow cards. Small disagreements** stay with the **on-field** crew.

Offside with VAR

Replays **freeze the moment of the pass** and draw **lines** on body parts that **count** (**head, body, feet—not arms**). A **goal** can be **disallowed** if any **scoring attacker** was **offside** when the **pass** was made.

Restarts after a change

- **Goal cancelled for offside:** an **indirect free kick** to the **defending team**.

- **Penalty given after review:** the restart is a **penalty kick**.

- **Red card after review:** the team plays with **fewer players**.

- **Play stopped but no offence:** the **referee** uses the **correct restart** (often a **dropped ball**).

Why it helps

Close offside, hidden handball, or a **missed red** card can **change a match**. VAR aims to **fix the big ones**, not to **re-referee everything**.

> **FACT:** VAR doesn't change the Laws—it helps apply them in tight, match-changing moments.

3.11 FAIR PLAY AND RESPECT

Play hard, play smart and play fair. **Respect** turns a match into a game everyone wants to play again.

Respect the referee: final say, calm voices

Listen to the **whistle** and **get on with it. No shouting, no crowding** the **referee**. If something needs **clarity**, the **captain** asks **politely** at a stoppage. **Decisions won't change** because players **argue**.

Play the ball, not the player: safety first

Tackle for the ball, not the legs. Late, reckless or **studs-up** challenges **risk a yellow or red card** and **injury**. If someone **falls**, check they're **OK** and **step back** so the **referee** can **see**.

Win with class, lose with grace: no taunting

Celebrate with your team, not at opponents. No mocking, no time-wasting, no kicking the ball away. Handshakes at the end show the **contest is over**.

Inclusion and language: everyone is welcome

No **insults** about **race, gender, disability, religion or background—ever. Kind words** build **strong teams; abusive words** bring **cards** and **spoil the game**.

Restarts and sportsmanship: do the right thing

Don't **block free kicks; retreat 9.15 metres** quickly. If play **stops for an injury** and your team **benefits** from the **restart** in a strange way, **returning the ball shows good sportsmanship** (the **Laws of the Game** often return it via a **dropped ball**).

Coaches and grown-ups: lead the tone

Coaches guide from the **technical area** and **model respect**. **Team officials** can be **cautioned** or **sent off** for **bad behaviour. Players** stay **focused** on the **pitch**.

> **FACT**: Removing a shirt to celebrate is a cautionable offence. Team officials, not just players, can also receive yellow and red cards.

CHAPTER 4
POSITIONS AND ROLES

Imagine your team as a **band**. Everyone has an **instrument**, everyone keeps the **rhythm**, and when it all clicks... **goal music!** In football, each **position** has a **job** that fits together like **puzzle pieces**. Some players **sprint down the wings**, some **knit passes** in **midfield**, and one brave soul wears **gloves** and says, '**Nothing gets past me.**' In this chapter, we'll meet every **role** on the **pitch** and show you what to watch for so you can spot each player's **superpower** during a match.

> <u>SPOT IT:</u> **While you read, think of your favourite team. Can you point at the TV (or on the pitch) to where each position usually plays?.**

4.1 GOALKEEPER (GK)

If the team is a **castle**, the **goalkeeper** is the **drawbridge—last to fall, first to shout**, and always **ready**. They're the only player allowed to use their **hands** (inside their **penalty area**), and their job is simple to say but tough to do: **keep the ball out of the net**.

What the GK does (in plain talk)

- **Shot-stopper: Catches, blocks**, or **tips** away any ball headed for **goal**.

- **Angle boss: Steps** forward or sideways to make the goal look '**smaller**' to the shooter.

- **Air traffic controller: Leaps** to **catch** or **punch** away high **crosses**.

- **First passer: Starts attacks** with **quick** throws, rolls, or passes after a save.

- **Team talker: Organises defenders**—'Mark No. 9!' 'Push up!' 'Keeper's ball!'

Home base and hand rules

- The **penalty area** is the **safe-hands zone**. The **GK** can use **their hands** anywhere **inside** it.

- **Outside the box? Feet only.** Once out, they become another **outfield player**.

- **No handling a team-mate's deliberate kick.** If a **defender deliberately** kicks it back, the **GK must use their feet** (headers or **deflections** from **team-mates** are **OK**)

Ready stance (look for this)

- **Feet light, knees bent, hands up**: like a **spring** ready to **pop**.

- **Eyes on the ball**: tiny steps to stay **balanced** before the shot (**set position**).

- **Catching shapes:** 'W' hands behind the ball high; 'basket' catch low.

Moving like a keeper

- **Sidestep, don't hop:** sidesteps keep the body **square** to the ball.

- **Close the angle:** step **towards** the shooter to **shrink** their target.

- **Dive with purpose: reach** to the ball; **land safely on their side or shoulder**.

- **Claiming crosses: jump strongly, knee up** for **protection**, shout 'Keeper!'

With the ball (start the attack!)

- **Quick throw or roll: fast counter** when **wingers** are **free**.

- **Side-foot pass: build from the back**, keep it **simple** and **safe**.

- **Goal kicks** can go **short** to **defenders** or **long** to the striker—**choose wisely**.

- **Sweeper-keeper moments: rush out** to clear **danger** behind the **defence**.

Mindset of a GK

- **Brave and calm: stand tall** in 1v1s; **shake off mistakes** quickly.

- **Loud leader: clear, short calls**—everyone **hears**, everyone **moves**.

- **Focus machine: concentrate** even when the ball is **far away**.

4.2 CENTRE-BACKS (CB)

If the goalkeeper is the **drawbridge**, the **centre-backs** are the **castle walls**—**solid**, **smart** and **built to last**. They live in the **middle** of the **back line** and make **danger** disappear.

What CBs do

- **Block the road:** Win **tackles** and get in the way of **shots**.

- **Win the air: Head** away **long balls** and **crosses** like it's their job (because it is).

- **Mark the threats:** Stick **close** to **strikers**, **track runners** into the **penalty area**.

- **Hold the line:** Keep **defenders** in a **straight line** to catch **attackers offside**.

- **Start the build-up: Pass calmly** into **midfield** or **switch play** to the **opposite wing**.

Home base and shape

- **Middle of the defence:** Between the **full-backs**, protecting the **penalty area** (the **box**).

- **Pairs work in tandem:** One **steps** to **challenge**; the other **covers** space **behind**.

- **Body angle: Half-turned**—ready to **sprint** either way.

How they defend

- **Jockey first, tackle second: Delay**, wait for a **heavy touch**, then **step in**.

- **Front-foot reads: Anticipate** the pass and **intercept it** before it **arrives**.

- **Box defending:** Stay between **the ball** and **the goal**; **block** with the **front foot** and stay **balanced**.

- **Set-pieces: Attack the ball** on **corners** and **free kicks** (at **both ends!**).

With the ball

- **Simple beats flashy: Side-foot passes** into the **No. 6** or **No. 8**, then **get set** again.

- **Switch it: Play a long diagonal** to **flip the play** when one side is **crowded**.

- **Break a line:** When **space opens, carry the ball forward** to draw out a **midfielder**.

Mindset of a CB

- **Calm captain energy: Organise** the **back line**—'**Step! Squeeze! Hold!**'

- **Brave, body-on-the-line defending: Blocks, headers, last-ditch slides** (timed, not wild).

- **Short memory: Concede? Reset.** Next **duel, win it**.

4.3 FULL-BACKS AND WING-BACKS

Meet the team's **touchline specialists**—part **defenders**, part **sprinters**, part **cross-makers**. They own the **edges** of the **pitch** and turn **defence** into **fast attacks**.

What they do

- **1v1 stoppers:** Face tricky **wingers** and say, '**Not today.**'

- **Overlap engines: Sprint** around the winger to **receive** and **cross**.

- **Underlap sneaks: Cut inside** the winger to surprise the **defence**.

- **Crosses and cut-backs: Deliver the ball** into the **box** or **pull it back** to the **penalty spot**.

- **Back-post guards: Track** the **far-post** winger when **crosses come in** from the opposite side.

Full-backs vs wing-backs: quick compare

- **Full-back:** Plays in a **back four** (e.g. **4-3-3, 4-2-3-1**). More **balanced: defend first, attack when safe**.

- **Wing-back:** Plays in a **back five** or **back three** (e.g. **3-5-2, 3-4-3**). More **attacking: higher starting position, more crosses**.

Defending the wide channel

- **Jockey and show wide: Angle the body** to push the winger **towards the touchline**.

- **Don't dive in: Delay** until **help arrives; time the tackle** on a **heavy touch**.

- **Track runners: Follow** the **back-post attacker** into the **box**.

- **Press triggers: Step up** when the **pass is slow** or when the opponent **receives the ball** facing their **own goal**.

With the ball

- **First touch forward: Explode into space** when there is **grass ahead**.

- **Pick your delivery: Low cut-back** for **runners, lofted cross** for a **tall striker**.

- **Combine: Quick wall passes** with the **winger** or **No. 8** to **break lines**.

- **Inverted option:** Sometimes **tuck inside** next to the **No. 6** to help in **midfield**.

Mindset of a wide defender

- **Relentless engine: Up, back, up, back—repeat**.

- **Scanner: Check shoulders** for the winger **ghosting at the far post**.

- **Decision-maker: Cross now, dribble inside,** or recycle—**choose fast, choose right**.

4.4 DEFENSIVE MIDFIELDER (NO. 6)

Meet the team's **anchor**—the player who **ties everything together**. When **danger** appears, the **No. 6 steps in front of the defence** like a **shield**; when your team has the **ball**, the **No. 6** is the **steady pivot** everyone can **pass to**.

What the No. 6 does

- **Shields the back line: Blocks passes** into the **striker** and the **No. 10**.

- **Wins and recycles: Nicks the ball**, plays a **simple pass**, and **resets the attack**.

- **Switch-master: Spots** the **far-side winger** and **switches play** to **open space**.

- **Traffic controller: Points, talks,** and keeps **team-mates** in the **right spots**.

- **Cover for full-backs:** When a **full-back bombs forward**, the **No. 6 slides across** to **cover** the full-back's **lane**.

Defensive smarts

- **Screen, don't chase:** Stay **between the ball and your centre-backs**.

- **Body angle: Side-on** so you can **pounce left or right**.

- **Tackle timing: Jab a toe in** on a **heavy touch; don't dive in early**.

- **Interceptions: Read the pass** and **step in—steal it before it arrives**.

On the ball

- **Be the outlet: Show for passes** from **defenders**, then **take one touch** to **escape pressure**.

- **Keep it simple: Short passes** into the **No. 8s** or **full-backs; play the way you face**.

- **Turn and break lines:** When there's time, **receive on the half-turn** and **feed a forward**.

- **Switch quickly:** See a **crowded side? Ping it** to the **far wing**.

Mindset of a No. 6

- **Calm heartbeat:** Even when the game is **chaotic**, the **No. 6** stays **cool**.

- **Scanner: Constant head turns**—'Where's **pressure?** Where's the spare player?'

- **First to danger: Spot counters early** and **stop them safely** and **fairly**.

4.5 CENTRAL MiDFiELDERS (8S)

Think of the **No. 8s** as the team's **engines**—**up and down, here and there, connecting defence to attack**. They help the **No. 6 build play** and help the **forwards create chances**. **Box-to-box** magic!

What the No. 8s do

- **Link the lines: Combine** with the **No. 6, full-backs,** and **attackers** to move up the **pitch**.

- **Arrive in the box: Time late runs** for **cut-backs** and **rebounds**.

- **Press and pinch: Step up** to **win the ball high** and keep the opponents pinned back.

- **Carry through traffic: Dribble into space** to **draw defenders** and then **pass**.

- **Create triangles: Offer angles** so the **ball carrier** always has **two options**.

Defensive smarts

- **Press triggers: Jump** when a **pass is slow** or when the **opponent receives the ball** facing their **own goal**.

- **Cut passing lanes: Shade your run** to **block** the easy ball into their **playmaker**.

- **Tackle cleanly: Jockey, poke,** then **win the ball—stay on your feet**.

On the ball

- **One-touch combos: Wall passes** with **wingers** and **full-backs** to **break lines**.

- **Split passes: Slide a through ball** between **defenders** for a **runner**.

- **Carry and commit: Dribble at a defender** to **pull them out**, then **dish** to a **team-mate**.

- **Cross or cut-back:** From the **half-space, pick out** the **striker** or the **far-post winger**.

Mindset of a No. 8

- **Relentless engine: Sprint to support,** then **sprint to recover—repeat**.

- **Picture-maker:** Before the ball arrives, they already **know** the **next pass**.

- **Brave with purpose: Take risks** that **open the game,** not **wild gambles**.

4.6 ATTACKING MIDFIELDER (NO. 10)

The **No. 10** is your **lock-picker**—when **defences** shut the door, the **No. 10 finds the key**. They **float** between **midfield** and the **striker, sniffing out space** and **slipping passes** that make crowds **gasp**.

What the No. 10 does

- **Finds pockets: Stands between the lines** where defenders **aren't sure** who should **mark** them.

- **Creates chances:** Plays **through-balls, one-twos**, and clever **cut-backs** for **shots**.

- **Turns and drives: Receives on the half-turn** and **runs at the defence**.

- **Links the front: Combines** with **wingers** and the **No. 9** to **build quick attacks**.

- **Set-piece guile:** Takes **corners** or **free kicks**, or makes **decoy runs** to **open space**.

Defensive smarts

- **Press the pivot: Jump towards** the opponent's **holding midfielder** to **block easy passes**.

- **Shadow cover: Angle your run** to **block** the pass into their **No. 10** while **pressing the ball**.

- **Counter-press: Lose it? Win it back in five seconds**—**first bite**, then **drop** if **beaten**.

On the ball

- **Scan early: Peek over both shoulders** before the **pass arrives**.

- **Slip runners: Weight the pass** so the **striker** doesn't need to **break stride**.

- **Shoot when free:** If defenders **back off, strike low** and **on target**.

- **Wall passes: Bounce it round the corner** to release an **overlapping full-back**.

Mindset of a No. 10

- **Bold but tidy: Try the magic pass,** but **protect the ball** in **tight spaces**.

- **Tempo-setter: Slow to draw defenders, quick** to **punch the gap**.

- **Head up, heart calm: Big moments** need **cool decisions**.

4.7 WINGERS (NOS. 7 AND 11)

Think **jet engines** on the **edges. Wingers stretch the pitch** wide, **burst** past **defenders**, and **serve chances** into the **box**—or **cut inside** and **curl** one into the **top corner**.

What wingers do

- **Stretch and scare:** Stay **wide** to make the **pitch big,** then **explode 1v1**.

- **Beat your mark: Dribble outside** to **cross** or **inside** to **shoot**.

- **Serve the box: Whip crosses**, slide low **cut-backs**, or chip **far-post** teasers.

- **Back-post hunter: Arrive at the far post** to **tap in** crosses from the opposite side.

- **Press from the front: Close down full-backs** and force them **towards the touchline**.

Touchline vs inverted: quick compare

- **Traditional winger: Right-footed on the right side** (or **left-footed on the left**). **Hugs the touchline, hits crosses** on the run.

- **Inverted winger: Right-footed on the left side** (or **vice versa**). **Cuts inside** onto their **stronger foot** to **shoot** or **thread passes**.

Defending the wing

- **Jockey and funnel: Show** their **full-back towards the touchline**; **don't get spun inside**.

- **Track the overlap: Follow** their full-back's **run— switch off** and you **concede**.

- **Press triggers: Pounce** on **slow touches** or **hospital passes** back to the full-back.

On the ball

- **First touch forward: Knock it into space** and **race**. Use **body feints** and **step-overs**.

- **Pick the finish: Low cut-back** for **runners, driven cross** for **headers**, or **inside shot** when the **lane opens**.

- **Combine in triangles: One-two** with the **No. 10** or **underlapping No. 8** to **unlock the channel**.

- **Switch alert:** If **crowded, recycle** and **switch play** to the **free winger**.

Mindset of a winger

- **Fearless: Try the take-on again**—even if the last one **failed**.

- **Head-up delivery: Cross to a shirt**, not just an **area**.

- **Relentless returner: Sprint back** to help your **full-back**—**team first**, then **flair**.

4.8 STRIKER (NO. 9) AND FALSE NINE

Meet the **goal-hunters**. The classic **No. 9** lives on the **last defender's shoulder**, waiting to **burst through** and **finish**. The **false nine** is a clever twist—**drops into midfield** to **pull defenders out** and create **space** for **team-mates** to attack.

What the No. 9 does

- **Finish, finish, finish: One-touch shots, headers, tap-ins**, and **calm 1v1 finishes**.

- **Hold-up play: Receive with your back to goal, shield the ball, lay it off**, then **spin in behind**.

- **Time the run: Curve your run** to stay **onside; dart to the near post** for **crosses**.

- **Lead the press: Chase centre-backs, steer** the ball to one side, and **block** the pass into their **No. 6**.

What a false nine adds

- **Drops into pockets: Centre-backs** must **choose— follow** (leaving **space**) or **hold** (giving **time**).

- **Links the play: Quick wall passes** with the **No. 10** and **wingers**; invites **third-man runs**.

- **Creates lanes for wingers:** As the **false nine drops, wide players sprint** into the **gaps**.

With the ball

- **First touch decides: Out of feet means a shot**; a **tight touch means a lay-off**.

- **Pick finishes: Shoot across** the **goalkeeper, lift the ball** if the **goalkeeper** goes **early**, or **square it** for a **tap-in**.

- **Box movement: Start central, dash near,** or **peel far— change speeds** to **lose your marker**.

Mindset of a No. 9

- **Hungry: Miss one? Want the next one even more.**

- **Brave: Attack crosses** where **boots** and **heads** fly.

- **Clever: Watch the back line, time the break, stay just onside.**

4.9 CAPTAINS AND COMMUNICATION

Think of the **captain** as the team's **compass** and **volume knob**—**pointing the way** and **turning the talk up or down** when needed. But great teams **communicate as one**.

What captains do

- **Lead the huddle: Set the tone** before **kick-off** and after **big moments**.

- **Talk to the referee (politely): Ask questions, pass on messages, keep calm**.

- **Organise: Point, clap,** and **shout clear cues**—'Step!' 'Squeeze!' 'Mark No. 9!'.

- **Set-piece boss: Assign marks, set the wall,** choose **near- or far-post runners**.

- **Steady the ship:** When things **wobble, model calm, effort,** and **respect**.

Team communication (everyone's job)

- **Simple code words:** 'Man on!' (pressure), 'Time!' (you're free), 'Turn!' (face forward), 'Switch!' (go to the other side).

- **Hand signals and pointing: Quick signs** to **press, overlap** or **reset**.

- **Names first:** 'Amina—turn!' 'Omar—step!' Clear and quick beats **loud and long**.

- Body language: Thumbs-up, eye contact, quick nods signal trust and speed.

Mindset

- Respectful and firm: Strong voices, never rude.

- Solution-first: Don't moan; say what to do next.

- Together: One message, one team.

4.10 FORMATIONS AT A GLANCE

A **formation** is your team's **starting map**—where players **stand** when play **begins**. It **changes** in **attack** and **defence**, but this **snapshot** helps you **spot shapes** fast.

4-3-3 (back four, single No. 6, two No. 8s, two wingers, one No. 9)

- **Feels like: Width and press. Wingers** stretch the **pitch**; **No. 8s** support **both ends.**

- **Attacking picture: Full-backs overlap, No. 8s arrive late, crosses** and **cut-backs** galore.

- **Defensive picture:** Often becomes **4-1-4-1**—the **No. 6 screens, wingers drop** into **midfield.**

- **Best for:** Teams with **speedy wingers** and a **mobile No. 9.**

- **Kid tip:** Count **three** in the **front line,** spread **wide**—hello, **4-3-3.**

4-2-3-1 (back four, two pivots, a No. 10, two wingers, one No. 9)

- **Feels like: Balanced and tidy.** Two **holding midfielders** (the **'double pivot'**) **protect** and **pass**.

- **Attacking picture:** The **No. 10 finds pockets; full-backs fly; wingers cut inside** or **cross**.

- **Defensive picture:** Often **slides to 4-4-2** as the **No. 10 steps up** next to the **No. 9**.

- **Best for:** Teams with a **clever No. 10** and **solid midfield control**.

- **Kid tip: Spot two sitting midfielders** in front of the **defence**.

3-5-2 (three centre-backs, wing-backs, three central midfielders, two strikers)

- **Feels like: Strong spine** and **flying wings. Wing-backs** own the **touchlines**.

- **Attacking picture: Wing-backs deliver;** one **striker checks**, the other **spins in behind**.

- **Defensive picture: Drops into 5-3-2**, with **wing-backs** forming a **back five**.

- **Best for:** Teams with **powerful centre-backs** and **two complementary strikers**.

- **Kid tip:** If you see **three centre-backs** and **two strikers**, it's likely **3-5-2**.

4-4-2 (back four, flat four in midfield, two strikers)

- **Feels like: Simple and compact. Two lines of four**, plus **twin strikers.**

- **Attacking picture: Crosses** from **wide midfielders, quick combinations** between the **two No. 9s.**

- **Defensive picture: Tight two banks of four**—hard to **pass through the middle.**

- **Best for:** Teams that **counter fast** and **love crosses.**

- **Kid tip:** Count **two strikers side by side**—classic 4-4-2.

CHAPTER 5
TACTICS MADE EASY

Football tactics are like **chess** at **top speed**. **Pieces (players)** **zoom**, **spaces open and close**, and one **smart move** can turn into a **goal**. In this chapter, we'll turn **tricky buzzwords** into **kid-easy ideas** you can **see during a match**. We'll show you **where to look, what the patterns mean**, and how **little choices**—one **pass**, one **press**—change the whole game.

> **SPOT IT:** Next time you watch, don't ball-watch. Pick a team shape (back four? back three?) and track how it changes in attack vs in defence.

5.1 BUILD-UP PLAY (SHORT VS LONG)

Ever tried getting a snack from the fridge with a puppy chasing you? You need a **plan—zig here, fake there, past the chair**. **Build-up play** is a team's **plan** to move the **ball** from the **goalkeeper** to the **forwards without losing it**.

Two main routes

- **Short build-up ('playing out from the back').**

  Quick **passes on the floor: goalkeeper → centre-backs → No. 6/No. 8s → wingers/No. 10/No. 9.**

    - **Why do it?** Keep the ball, pull defenders out of shape, create gaps.

Keys: Triangles for easy options, **one-touch passes**, players **showing to feet**.

- **Long build-up ('go long')**.

  A **high pass** to the **striker** or **winger** to **gain territory** quickly.

  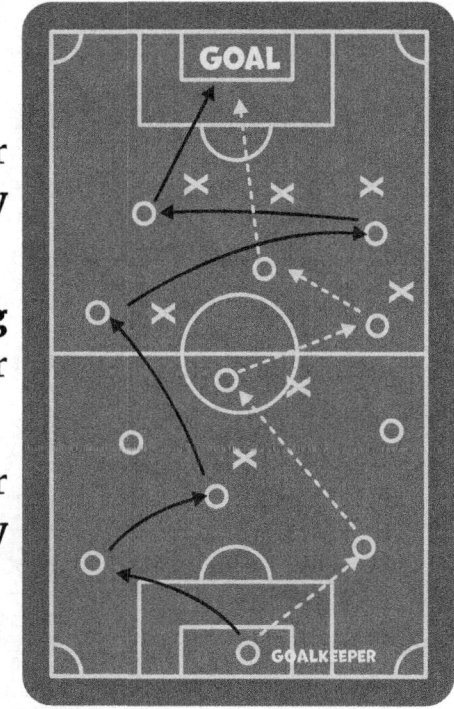

  - **Why do it?** Beat a strong **press**, use a **tall No. 9**, or counter quickly.

  - **Keys:** Good timing for **flick-ons**, **runners ready** for **second balls**.

Simple patterns you'll see

- **Split centre-backs and drop No. 6: Centre-backs** stand **wide**; the **No. 6 drops** to **receive**.

- **Full-back high, winger inside:** Creates a **passing lane** on the **outside**.

- **Third-man run: A to B**, B **plays a one-touch pass to C** **running through**.

- **Switch of play: Three or four passes** to **flip the ball** to the **free side**.

When to choose short vs long

- **Go short if:** Your **goalkeeper** and **defenders** are **calm**, the **press** is **light**, the **pitch** is **smooth**.

- **Go long if:** The **opponents press hard**, it's **rainy or bumpy**, or your **No. 9** is **winning everything**.

Tiny build-up wins

- **First touch forward:** Receive and **face the pitch**.
- **Body shape open:** Side-on so you can **pass either way**.
- **Don't force the centre:** If **crowded, recycle** and **switch**.

<u>Mini glossary</u>

- <u>Playing out:</u> **Building** with **short passes** from the back.
- <u>Second ball:</u> The **loose ball** after a **header** or challenge.
- <u>Break a line:</u> **Pass through** a row of **defenders** or midfielders.
- <u>Switch of play:</u> **Move the ball quickly** from one **wing** to the **other**.

5.2 PRESSING AND BLOCKS (HIGH, MID, LOW)

Pressing is like **team tag**: you **hunt together** to **win the ball back**. A **block** is where your team sets its **defensive line**—**high**, **mid**, or **low**.

The three blocks

- **High block:** Defend near the **opponents' penalty area**.

    - **Goal: Win it** close to their goal, which **creates quick chances**.
    - **Risk: Space behind** your **back line**.

- **Mid block:** Defend around the **halfway line**.

    - **Goal:** Be **compact** and **spring counters**.

- **Risk:** Being **too passive leads to easy passes** for them.

- **Low block:** Defend near **your penalty area**.

  - **Goal: Protect the goal; block shots and crosses.**
  - **Risk:** Harder to counter if **everyone is deep**.

Pressing triggers (when to pounce)

- **Bad touch** or **bobble** by a **defender**.

- **Back-pass** to the **goalkeeper (GK)** or a defender **facing their own goal**.

- **Pass to the touchline** (it **acts like an extra defender**).

- **Receiver on their weaker foot**.

- A **lofted ball** that **takes time to drop**.

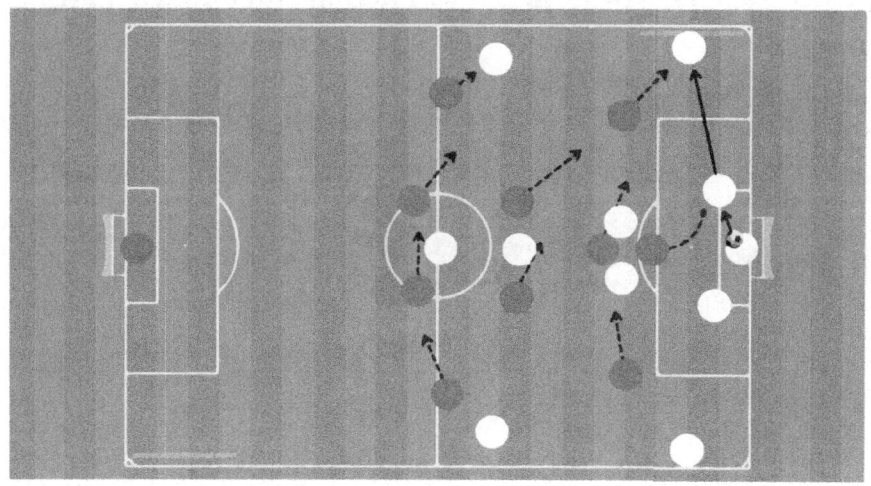

How to press (angles win!)

- **Curve your run: Hide the easy pass** with your **cover shadow**.

- **One goes, one covers:** First player **presses**; second **blocks the return pass**.

- **Trap a side: Guide** the ball to the **wing**, then **squeeze as a team**.

- **Stop the switch:** A **midfielder** sits in the **passing lane** to the **far side**.

High vs mid vs low: what it looks like

- **High press: Wingers jump** to **full-backs**, the **No. 9** **closes** a **centre-back**, the **No. 10 blocks** their **No. 6**.

- **Mid block: Two tight lines** (e.g. **4-4-2**), **shifting side to side, waiting for a trigger**.

- **Low block: Everyone behind the ball; clear headers, block shots**, then **counter with speed**.

After you win it (the bonus move)

- **Counter-attack: One or two quick passes** into **space** for **runners**.

- **Counter-press (five-second rule):** If you **lose it, sprint** to **win it back immediately before they can look up**.

Mini glossary

- **Block (high, mid, low):** Where a team sets its **defence** on the **pitch**.

- **Trigger:** A **signal** to **start pressing** (e.g. **bad touch, back-pass**).

- **Cover shadow:** The **passing lane** your **body blocks** while you **press**.

- **Trap: Steering** the ball into a **zone** your team is **ready to win**.

5.3 TRANSITIONS (COUNTER-ATTACK, COUNTER-PRESS)

Transitions are the **blink-and-you-miss-it** moments when the ball **changes possession** and everyone must **flip roles** instantly. The best sides treat these **five seconds** like **gold**.

When you **win the ball**, a **counter-attack races** into the **spaces** the other team left behind. **First pass forward** or **wide to a runner; team-mates burst beyond**, and the **shot** arrives **before defenders set their feet**. Think **lightning: few touches, big strides, brave decisions.**

When you **lose the ball**, a **counter-press** (also called **'gegenpressing'**) tries to **win it back immediately.** The **nearest players close the ball, team-mates block the closest passes**, and the **whole unit squeezes the area around the ball.** Either you **steal it back**, or you **force a panicked long ball** you can **mop up.**

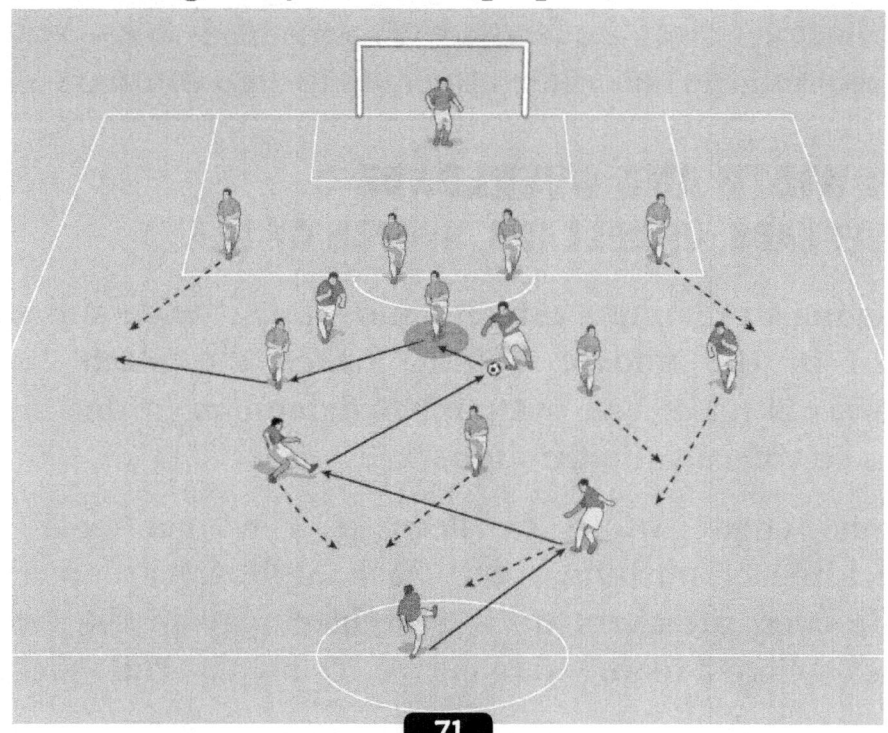

Quick cues (four to remember)

- **Win it? Head up, first pass forward, runners explode.**

- **No pass on? Carry into space,** then **slide a simple ball.**

- **Lose it? Three swarm: one presses, one blocks** the return, **one hunts** the next pass.

- **Press beaten? Drop quickly** into **shape—no heroes,** just **team speed.**

<u>**Mini glossary**</u>

- <u>**Transition:**</u> the **instant** when **possession changes.**

- <u>**Counter-attack:**</u> a **quick break** straight after **winning the ball.**

- <u>**Counter-press:**</u> **immediate team press** right after **losing it.**

- <u>**Rest defence:**</u> the **few players** your team **keeps ready behind the ball** while attacking to **stop counters.**

5.4 WIDTH AND OVERLOADS
(OVERLAPS, UNDERLAPS, SWITCH OF PLAY)

Imagine stretching a **rubber band**—pull it **wide** and **gaps open in the middle. Width** makes the **pitch huge; overloads** make you **outnumber defenders** in one small area so you can **slip through.**

Teams create **width** by keeping a **winger** near the **touchline** or pushing a **full-back high.** Once defenders **slide over,** attackers try a **switch of play** to the 'weak side', where a **team-mate** is **free.** To break a **full-back**

2v1, you'll see **overlaps** (run **around the outside**) and **underlaps** (dart **inside**, between **the full-back** and **the centre-back**). Both runs **force a choice**—whichever defender **hesitates first—loses**.

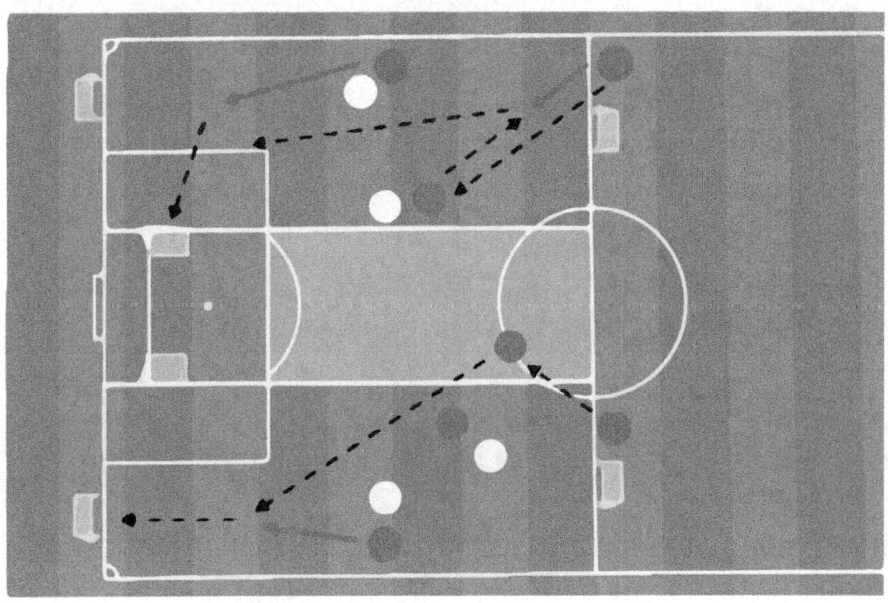

Quick cues (four to spot)

- **Winger hugs the touchline,** and the **full-back arrives at speed → overlap.**

- **Winger dribbles inside,** and the **No. 8 darts between defenders → underlap.**

- **Three close players** form a **triangle** and **pass quickly →** **overload.**

- **Crowd on one side?** The **ball zips across → switch of play** to the **free runner.**

5.5 SET-PiECE iDEAS
(CORNERS: ZONAL VS MAN-MARKiNG; FREE KiCKS)

Set-pieces are the **classroom plays** coaches draw the night before—**short, sharp plans** to **steal a goal** when the ball is **still**. **Corners** and **free kicks** work because **everyone knows the script**—and then one **player** does something **unexpected**.

For **corners**, teams choose how to **defend the box**. In man-marking, each **defender sticks to a runner**. In zonal, **defenders guard spots (front zone, penalty spot, back zone)** and **attack the ball** when it **enters**. Many teams use a **mixed version**: a few **zonal anchors** plus **man-markers** for the **biggest threats**. Attackers try **near-post flicks**, **screens** (legal body positions—no pushing) to **free a team-mate**, or a **short corner** to **change the angle** before **crossing**.

For **free kicks, direct shots bend** or **dip** over the **wall**, while **wide free kicks** are basically **'crosses in disguise'**.

One player may **run over the ball** as a **decoy**, another **nudges it**, and the **striker darts across the line** at just the **right beat**. The

goalkeeper sets the wall, the **captain checks marks**, and then it's all about **timing** and **delivery**.

Quick cues (four to spot)

- **Corner-taker's hand signal:** which **routine** is coming (**near post, far post, short**).
- **One attacker sprints near post**, and **another peels far post** at the **last second**.
- **On defence, a tall player guards the front zone**; others go **goal side** of their **mark**.
- **After the first header,** watch the **edge-of-the-box player shoot the second phase**.

Mini glossary

- <u>**Zonal and man-marking:**</u> guarding spaces vs guarding opponents at **set-pieces**.

- <u>**Inswinger and outswinger:**</u> **corner** bending **towards** or **away from goal**.

- <u>**Near-post flick:**</u> a **glancing header** that **redirects the ball** across **goal**.

- <u>**Second phase:**</u> **play** after the **first header** or **clearance** from a **set-piece**.

5.6 CREATING CHANCES
(CUT-BACKS, CROSSES, THROUGH-BALLS)

Scoring is the **finish**; **chance creation** is the **recipe**. Good teams mix three main **flavours**—**cut-backs, crosses,** and **through-balls**—and **choose** the one the **defence** leaves **open**.

When a **winger** bursts to the **byline**, a **cut-back** becomes king: the ball is **pulled to the penalty spot** for a **late-arriving No. 8 or No. 10** to **strike**. When **defenders sit deep and narrow**, the **outside** is open—time for **crosses: driven low** for **runners, whipped** at **head height** for the **No. 9,** or **floated** to the **far post** for the **far winger.** If the **back line steps high,** the **space is behind**—perfect for a **through-ball slipped** between legs or **chipped** over a desperate foot. The **No. 9 curves the run** to stay **onside;** the **No. 10 weights the pass so that** no extra **touches** are needed.

Small patterns help: an **overlap** to **free a clean crossing angle;** an **underlap** to **surprise the full-back;** a **quick one-two** in the **half-space** to **unlock a lane. Head up, choose quickly, and hit the team-mate, not just the area.**

Quick cues (four to spot)

- **Ball near the byline?** Expect a **low cut-back** to the **penalty spot**.

- **Box crowded? Winger recycles,** and the team makes a **switch of play** to the **free side**.

- **High line?** Watch the **No. 10 slip the No. 9 through** with a **perfectly timed run.**

- **Cross coming?** The **No. 9 darts to the near post**, the **far winger ghosts to the far post**, and the **No. 10 waits at the edge of the box**.

> <u>Mini glossary</u>
>
> - <u>**Cut-back:**</u> a **low pass** pulled back from near the **byline** to a **shooter**.
>
> - <u>**Through-ball:**</u> a **pass** threaded **past or over defenders** for a **runner**.
>
> - <u>**Half-space:**</u> **channel** between **centre** and **wing**—great for **combinations**.
>
> - <u>**Far post:**</u> the **goalpost furthest** from the point from which the ball is delivered.

5.7 GAME MANAGEMENT
(TEMPO, SUBSTITUTIONS, CLOSING OUT)

Great teams don't just **play**; they **manage moments**. **When to speed up, when to breathe, when to change shape**—these choices quietly **decide tight matches**.

Tempo is your **heartbeat. Fast tempo—quick throws, quick free kicks, one-touch passing**—can **rattle a defence. Slow tempo—three passes, open the body, switch sides**—can **calm a storm** and **waste the opposition's energy. Coaches** nudge tempo with simple cues: 'Two touches!', 'Switch!', or by **moving a midfielder deeper** to **keep the ball**.

Substitutions are **levers. A fresh winger** late on means new **sprints against tired legs**; an **extra centre-back** adds **height** to **defend crosses**; a **creative No. 10 chases a goal**.

Subs also **change shape**—for example, from **4-3-3** to **4-4-2**—to match what the **game state** demands, not just what the **line-up** said at **kick-off**.

Closing out means **finishing the job. Protect the centre,** keep **full-backs sensible, win the first balls** and—just as important—**the second balls. Use the ball to rest: three passes, switch, repeat. Attack the spaces** that make the other team **nervous**, not the ones that make **you tired**.

Quick cues (four to remember)

- **Protect the centre; show opponents to the wings.**
- **When leading: simple passes, big clearances, smart fouls (but fair).**
- **When chasing: add runners, raise tempo, press on triggers.**
- **Last minutes: mark tightly on set-pieces; one player stays high to stretch them.**

Mini glossary

- **Tempo:** how **fast** a team **moves the ball.**
- **Game state:** what the **score and time demand (1–0 up versus 0–1 down).**
- **Shape:** the team's **positioning without the ball.**
- **Second ball:** the **loose ball** after an **aerial duel** or **tackle.**

FACT: Under IFAB Law 7, the referee must add time at the end of each half to compensate for delays—substitutions, injuries, disciplinary sanctions, goal celebrations, VAR checks/reviews, and other stoppages. So making lots of late subs to slow the game doesn't reduce the clock; it often increases stoppage time.

5.8 DATA WORDS YOU HEAR (KiD-LEVEL)

Data is just a **story in numbers**. **Analysts** turn a **match** into **simple pictures** that help **coaches** and **players** make **better choices**.

xG (expected goals) estimates **how likely** a **shot** is to **become a goal**, based on **where** and **how** it was taken. A **tap-in** might be **0.7** (great chance); a **long shot** might be **0.03** (rare). **Team xG** adds up **all shots** to show **whether** you **created enough** to score.

Heat maps colour the pitch to show **where** a **player** or **team** spent the **most time**. A **big red blob** on the **right wing**? Your **winger lived there. Pass maps show who passed to whom** and **how often**—**thick lines mean favourite routes**.

Other friendly numbers: possession (time on the ball), **shots on target**, **pressures** (how often you **pressed/closed down** the **ball** or **ball-carrier**), **progressive passes** (balls that actually **move you up the pitch towards goal**). **None** are **perfect**; **together** they make the **picture clearer**.

Quick cues (four to remember)

- **High xG, low goals means finishing cold**; **low xG, many goals means finishing hot**.

- **Heat map wide and high indicates attacking width**; **low and central indicates a low block**.

- **Pass map thick to full-backs means build wide**; **thick into the No. 10 means play between the lines**.

- **Compare first half versus second half** maps to see **tactical tweaks**.

Mini glossary

- **xG: a shot's chance of becoming a goal (0 to 1)**.

- **Heat map: a picture of where play happened most**.

- **Pass map: who connects with whom, and how often**.

- **Progressive pass: a ball** that **meaningfully moves you towards goal**.

5.9 FOOTBALL TECH AND THE FUTURE

Modern football uses **clever tools** to help **fair calls** and **smart training**—and most of it works **quietly in the background**.

Goal-line technology answers one question: **did the whole ball cross the whole line?** Multiple **high-speed cameras** track the ball; if it's **in**, the **referee's watch** gives an **instant signal**.

Semi-automated offside (SAOT) uses **cameras** (and sometimes **sensors**) to track **players' body points**. The system **suggests offside or onside** with a quick visual; the **refereeing team confirms it**. It's still **humans in charge**— the **tech** just **speeds up the decision**.

VAR (Video Assistant Referee) is a **replay helper** for **clear and obvious errors** on **four things: goals, penalties, direct red cards**, and **mistaken identity**. It **does not re-referee** the whole match; it **checks big, match-changing moments**.

GPS vests and tracking measure **distance, top speed, sprints**, and how hard you **decelerate**, so **coaches** can **adjust training loads** and **reduce injury risk**. Camera **tracking** follows **every player** to study **pressing, spacing**, and **set-piece movement**.

What analysts do: cut short clips, tag events (e.g. **pressing triggers, third-man runs**), and share **simple notes** players can use: **'Show them wide', 'Switch earlier', 'Arrive later at the box'**. The best **analysis** sounds like a **clear cue**, not a **maths lecture**.

Quick cues (four to spot)

- **Referee points to the wrist: goal-line technology confirmed**.
- **Long offside delay, then signal: technology check** before the **flag**.
- **Referee goes to the monitor: potential VAR review** on a **big decision**.
- **Players wearing tight vests in training: GPS trackers** are on.

CHAPTER 6

SKILLS & SMART HABITS (EXPLAINED, NOT COACHED)

Think of your game like a **toolbox**. You don't need a **thousand tricks**—you need the **right tool** at the **right moment**. In this chapter, we'll explain the **habits** great players lean on every day: **how they shape their bodies, how they choose a pass**, and how **tiny choices** make football feel **easier**.

> **SPOT IT:** Watch any good team for five minutes. You'll notice the same **quiet habits** popping up—**head turns** before the ball, **first touches into space, simple passes** to the **safe side**. That's 'smart' football.

6.1 FIRST TOUCH AND BODY SHAPE

Your **first touch** is the **opening move** of every **passage of play**. **Get it right** and the next **pass, dribble**, or **shot** becomes **simple**.

When the ball comes, think '**arrive early, open early**'. Take a few **light steps** to **meet it**, set your **feet side-on (half-turn)**, and **let the ball roll** where you want to go. A **cushion touch** (soft—**absorb with the instep**) keeps the ball **close**; a **set touch** (a **firmer push**) moves it into **space** so your **second action** is **ready**. Use the **foot furthest from the defender** to **protect** the ball, and keep your **arms out** for **balance** and to **feel pressure** (not to push).

Before the ball even **starts travelling**, do what **professionals ('pros')** do: **scan. Quick head turns**—**left, right, back to the ball**—tell you **who's near, who's free**, and **which way is safe**. Now your **first touch** has a **destination**, not a **guess**.

Quick cues (three to remember)

- **Open your body (half-turn)** so you can **play forward** in **one touch**.

- **Touch to the safe side** (away from pressure), then **look up**.

- **Meet the ball—don't wait for it**—so **you control the bounce**, not the other way round.

> **FACT:** **Top players scan** (look around) **several times before the ball reaches them.** Seeing the **pitch** early is a **real skill that coaches measure**, not just a **good habit**.

Mini glossary

- **Half-turn (side-on):** body **angled** so you can see the **ball** and the **pitch**.

- **Cushion touch: soft first touch** to slow and **control** the ball.

- **Set touch:** a firmer **first touch** that **places the ball** for your **next action**.

- **Far foot:** the **foot furthest from the defender**, used to **protect possession**.

6.2 PASSING CHOICES

Passing is choosing the best **route**. Sometimes you take the **near** street (**short**), sometimes a **motorway** (**long**), sometimes a **hidden shortcut** (**through**), and sometimes you drive **around traffic** (**switch**).

Short passes keep the ball and pull defenders out of shape. **Aim for** your team-mate's **back foot** (the one that faces forward) so they can play **quickly**.

Long passes win **territory** or **skip a press** – use them when a **winger** or **striker** has space and you can hit a **clean, flat strike** or a **gentle clip**.

Through-balls slice behind a **high line**. Wait for your runner to be **level** (onside), then **weight** the pass so they don't **break stride**.

Switches move the ball from a **crowded** side to the **weak** side. **Two or three safe passes** – or **one diagonal** – turn **pressure** into **freedom**.

How do you choose? Head up: picture it early, then **commit**. If the **centre** is jammed, **recycle** and **switch**. If a team-mate calls '**time!**', **use it** to **turn** or **punch** a **forward pass**. If the **runner** has **gone – trust your technique** and **play them in**.

Quick cues (three to remember)

- **Back foot** = **faster next touch**.

- If one side is **crowded**, **switch** – don't **force** it through bodies.

- See the **run**? Play into **space**, not to **feet**.

> **FACT:** A **firm pass** can travel **about 1.5 seconds** over **thirty metres**; even a **fast sprinter** needs **more than three seconds** to cover that. The **ball** usually **beats the runner** – **use it**.

Mini glossary

- **Back foot:** The receiver's foot that faces the **direction** they want to go.

- **Through-ball:** A pass **threaded behind defenders** for a **runner**.

- **Switch of play:** Moving the ball **quickly** to the **opposite wing**.

- **Weak side:** The **far side** with **fewer defenders** after a **shift**.

6.3 DRIBBLING DECISIONS

Dribbling isn't a dance show – it's a **key**. Use it to open **space**, not to collect **moves**.

Ask yourself a quick **triple-check** before you go: **Space? Speed? Support?** If there's **space** to attack, you're already moving at **speed**, and a **team-mate** is in **support** if you're stopped – **go for it**. If **two defenders** are closing or a

team-mate is **free and facing forward, pass and move** instead.

Good dribbles **start early**. Take a **positive first touch** towards the **gap, shape** your body like you might **pass**, then **change of pace** (slow to fast) or **change of direction** (inside to outside) to unbalance the defender. Keep the ball on your **far foot** and use your **arm for balance**  **and feel** (not pushing). **Most importantly,** have an **exit** ready in your head – a **cross**, a **cut-back**, a **shot**, or a simple **lay-off**.

Quick cues (three to remember)

- If the defender's **feet are square, burst past**; if they're **side-on, cut back.**

- **Beat one?** Decide **instantly** – **pass, cross,** or **shoot** before help arrives.

- **No room? Recycle** and try the **opposite side** – your **run still pulls defenders**.

> <u>FACT:</u> At higher levels, most successful **take-ons** begin with the attacker already **moving at the defender. Speed** forces the **mistake** more often than **tricks** alone.

6.4 SHOOTING CHOICES

The **goal** looks huge until a **goalkeeper** fills your brain. **Calm the picture:** pick a **corner** first, then **swing**.

From **wide angles**, shooting **across the goalkeeper** (towards the **far post**) is powerful: if it doesn't go in, it often creates a **rebound** for **team-mates**. At **tight angles**, the goalkeeper protects the **near post**, so a quick **near-post** hit can **surprise** them – especially if struck **early, low,** and **hard**. From **central areas, open your body** and **pass** the ball into the **corner** with the **instep,** or **drive with the laces** when you need **power**.

Your **set-up** matters more than your **power. Plant your foot so it points** where you want to finish; **keep your head**

still; **keep your ankle firm**. Keep most shots **low – grass-level** goals are common and **rebounds are friendlier**. And always **follow in – taps** from **spills** win matches.

Quick cues (three to remember)

- **Wide angle?** Go **far post**: **low across the goal** for either **a goal** or **a rebound**.

- **Keeper cheats near?** Snap a **near-post** shot **early** before they **set themselves**.

- **Edge of the box? Open the body** and **pass it** into the **corner**.

FACT: Goalkeepers are trained to **guard the near post** first on **tight angles**. **Shooting across goal** not only **tests** them but also creates **tap-in rebounds** for **onrushing team-mates**.

Mini glossary

- **Near post / Far post:** The **post closest** to the **shooter** / the one **further away**.

- **Across the goalkeeper: Shot aimed past** the goalkeeper **towards the far post**.

- **First-time finish: Shooting** without a **controlling touch**.

- **Rebound:** A **loose ball** after the goalkeeper **saves** but **can't hold**.

6.5 HEADING SAFETY (FOLLOW LOCAL GUIDANCE)

Your **brain** matters more than any goal. If your age group limits or bans heading, follow your coach and local rules. When heading is allowed, think 'safe habits first, technique second'.

Safe headers **meet** the ball; they don't let it smack them. See it early, take small steps, and **jump and strike with your forehead** (the flat area just above your eyebrows).  Keep your **eyes open**, your neck firm, your core braced, and your **elbows down** for balance (not swinging). Use the right ball size and pressure, and avoid old, **waterlogged** balls that feel heavy. If the situation is crowded, or low to the ground near players' boots, don't put your head there — use your **chest** or **foot** instead.

Quick cues (three to remember)

- If heading is permitted, **forehead contact**, eyes open, neck firm.

- **Meet** the ball in the air; don't let it hit you.

- **Elbows down**; land balanced. If unsure, use your chest or foot.

6.6 MOVEMENT OFF THE BALL

Most of football is played **without the ball**. Great players **move** before the pass exists, creating **space** for team-mates and arriving at the perfect moment.

Think in **pairs**: one player stretches the defence (runs long or wide), another shows **short** to receive. Offer **angles** — left, right, and behind the ball — so the passer has simple choices. Use little double movements (away to back, slow to fast) to lose a marker. After you pass, **move again**: **one-two**, spin in behind, or drift to a new pocket so you're always useful.

Quick cues (three to remember):

- **Two options:** one to feet (short), one into **space** (long).

- **Drag then dash:** move a defender one way, then burst the other.

- **Pass and move:** don't admire your pass — go again to support.

FACT: Players spend far more time **off the ball** than on it — your positioning and runs often create the chance even if you never touch the pass.

Mini glossary

- **Check to:** Quick step **towards** the ball to receive under control.

- **Run in behind:** Sprint past the back line into **space**.

- **Third-man run:** Two combine so a third **team-mate** breaks through.

- **Decoy run:** A purposeful run that moves defenders to free a **team-mate**.

6.7 COMMUNICATION & RESPECT

Football is a team puzzle. The faster you **share** the picture, the faster your team **solves** it. **Clear** words, **kind** habits, and **respect** for everyone — team-mates, opponents, referees — turn good players into a great team.

Keep your messages **short** and useful: 'Man on!', 'Time!', 'Turn!', 'Switch!', 'Step!', 'Hold!' Say the **name** first, then the **action**: '**Mike, time!**' Use gestures too — point early, **give a thumbs-up** after a mistake, clap to encourage the next effort. Respect is **active**, not silent: help an opponent up, hand the ball back for a **throw-in**, and let the **captain** do the talking if the team needs to ask the **referee** something.

Quick cues (three to remember):

- **Name and action:** 'Omar, switch!' (clear and quick beats loud and long).

- **One message** at a time: give the next action, not a lecture.

- **Respect first:** no moaning; **listen**, **nod**, play on.

> **FACT:** Teams that communicate with **short, specific** cues (name and action) make decisions **faster** than teams that rely on general shouting — **clarity beats volume**.

Mini glossary

- **Code words:** Shared short calls for common actions ('Time', 'Turn', 'Switch').

- **Call:** A quick instruction to help a **team-mate**.

- **Captain:** The player who leads talks with team-mates and, when needed, speaks to the referee.

- **Sportsmanship:** Respect in action — **fair play**, helping others up, shaking hands.

6.8 THE MENTAL GAME

Your **brain** is your best boot. **Confidence** isn't magic; it's a set of small **habits** you repeat so often they feel normal — before the **kick-off**, after a mistake, and in big moments.

Build a simple **reset**: one breath **in** (count to **four**), one long breath **out** (count to **six**), shoulders down, and **eyes up**. Use helpful **self-talk**: 'Next play', 'Strong touch', 'Find the pass'. Treat mistakes like speed bumps — **feel it, fix it, forget it**. Confidence grows when you do the **basics** well: **scan** early, first touch to the **safe side**, **pass with purpose**. Big games don't need new tricks; they need your **good habits**, done again.

Quick cues (three to remember):

- **Breathe, then words, then action:** reset, say a cue ('next play'), do the next simple thing.

- **Eyes up, body up:** positive body language helps you and your team.

- **Park the error:** learn fast, then move on — don't replay it in your head.

FACT: A slow exhale activates your body's calming system (parasympathetic response), which can steady your heart rate and sharpen decisions in the next few seconds.

Mini glossary

- **Self-talk:** Short, helpful phrases you say to guide your next action.

- **Next-play mentality:** Let the last moment go — focus on what's now.

- **Body language:** How you stand and move; it affects confidence and **team-mates**.

- **Reset breath:** A deliberate inhale–exhale pattern to calm and refocus.

6.9 REST & RECOVERY

Training makes you tired; **recovery** makes you better. Muscles, brain, and mood all improve when you treat **rest** like part of the plan, not an optional extra. (*This section is non-medical advice.*)

Before activity, use **dynamic** movements (a light jog, skips and hip circles) to warm joints and wake muscles. **After** activity, slow to a walk, **breathe**, then use easy **static stretches** (hold gently; no bouncing) to tell your body, '**job done**'. The biggest recovery tool isn't fancy — it's **sleep**. A steady **bedtime**, a **calm room**, and **screens off** a little earlier make tomorrow's touch cleaner and choices faster. If you're hurt or feel unwell, stop and tell a **parent or coach**.

Quick cues (three to remember):

- **Warm up** dynamically, **cool down** gently — move first, then hold.

- **Protect sleep:** the same bedtime, a calm room, screens off earlier.

- **Water** and easy **food** after play to **refuel** and **rehydrate**.

> **FACT:** During **sleep**, your brain strengthens new skills and memories, so yesterday's practice is easier to repeat today.

6.10 FOOD AND HYDRATiON BASiCS

Food is fuel, not a fuss. You don't need special diets: just regular meals with colour on the plate and **water first**.

A good rule: build a **balanced plate** — some **fruit and veg**, a serving of starchy carbs (rice, pasta, potatoes or bread), and a serving of **protein** (eggs, beans, fish, chicken, dairy or alternatives). On busy days, simple snacks help: fruit, yoghurt or a small sandwich. Sip water through the day and bring a bottle to training. For most kids and most sessions, **water is enough**. Ask a **parent or coach** before using sports drinks. Don't try brand-new foods right before a match — save experiments for another day.

Quick cues (three to remember):

- **Water first**; sip often; bring your bottle.

- **Balanced plate:** fruit and veg, carbs and protein.

- **Familiar foods** on match day; new foods later.

> **FACT:** Even mild dehydration can make running feel harder and decisions slower — **regular sips** help you think and move better.

CHAPTER 7

COMPETITIONS, CLUBS AND PATHWAYS

Football isn't just one big league — it's a busy map of **seasons**, **cups**, ladders and teams all moving at once. This chapter is your friendly guide: how a league race works, why cup nights feel different, what **'fixtures'** and **'tables'** actually show, and how to read them like a pro in seconds.

> **SPOT IT:** On any **given weekend**, one team might chase points in the **league** and, midweek, risk everything in a **cup**. Same players, different **pressure**.

7.1 LEAGUE V CUP (POINTS V KNOCKOUTS)

Think of a **league** as a **marathon** and a **cup** as a **sprint**.

In a league, teams play everyone (usually **home and away**) and collect points across the whole season — **three** for a **win**, **one** for a **draw**. The most points at the end **wins** the title, while places near the bottom can mean **relegation** (we'll get there soon).

A cup is **knockout**: lose and you're **out**. Some rounds are **one match**; some are **two legs** (home and away). If it's level after normal time, competitions may use **extra time** and then **penalties** to find a winner. That's why cup games feel like **cliffhangers** — one goal can flip everything.

Quick cues (three to remember):

- **League = consistency:** many matches, points add up, steady form wins.

- **Cup = jeopardy:** one bad night? **Out.** One great night? **Through.**

- **Different tactics:** rotate in leagues; go bold or be cautious in cups — **it depends on the tie**.

> **SPOT IT:** Notice how managers **rest** players in a busy league week but start their **strongest XI** on a big cup night. The **risk** level changes the choices.

> **FACT:** Most leagues worldwide use **three points** for a win and **one** for a draw, which **rewards attacking play** over settling for draws.

7.2 FIXTURES AND TABLES

A **fixture** is simply a scheduled match — date, time, **home and away**. A **table** is the season's scoreboard: P (played), W (wins), D (draws), L (losses), GF/GA (goals **for and against**), GD (**goal difference**), and Pts (points). With a quick glance, you can see who's **flying**, who's wobbling, and who needs a result next weekend.

Fans also read the **form line** (last **five** matches, often shown as W/D/L entries) and talk about the **run-in** — the final stretch of fixtures that can decide titles, European spots, or survival. A tough run-in might mean multiple away games or several top opponents in a row; an easier one might be **home-heavy** against lower teams. Tables don't tell the whole story — but they tell **a lot**.

> **FACT:** In many leagues, **goal difference** is the first **tiebreaker** when teams finish level on points, which encourages teams to keep pushing for **one more goal**.

7.3 PROMOTION AND RELEGATION

Seasons feel exciting because ladders move. Finish **high** and you go **up** a division; finish **low** and you go **down**. That's **promotion** and **relegation** — simple idea, huge drama.

Most divisions send a set number up **automatically** (often the top one or two). Then come the **play-offs**: a short, **end-of-season** mini-tournament for teams just below the automatic places. **Winners of the semi-finals** meet in a **one-off final** that decides the last promotion place. At the other end, the teams at the **bottom** drop to the division below. The exact numbers **vary by league**, but the feeling is the same: **every point matters**.

Quick cues (three to remember):

- **Top rises, bottom drops:** places near the **top and bottom** matter most.

- **Play-offs mean an extra ticket up:** finish close to the top to get a **second chance**.

- **Goal difference can save you:** one extra **goal** across a season can **flip positions**.

7.4 THE ENGLISH LEAGUE PYRAMID

Picture a **pyramid** of leagues joined by little bridges. At the top sits the top division, the **Premier League**. Below it are three national tiers run by the English Football League: the **Championship** (2nd level), **League One** (3rd), and **League Two** (4th). Under those, the **National League** (5th) and then two regional divisions—National League North and South (6th)—lead into many local leagues as the pyramid widens.

Why '**pyramid**'? Because each step down has more clubs, spread across regions, but all connected by **promotion** and **relegation**. A small club can climb step by step over years; a big club can also fall if results go wrong. It's one giant **ladder**, open at both ends.

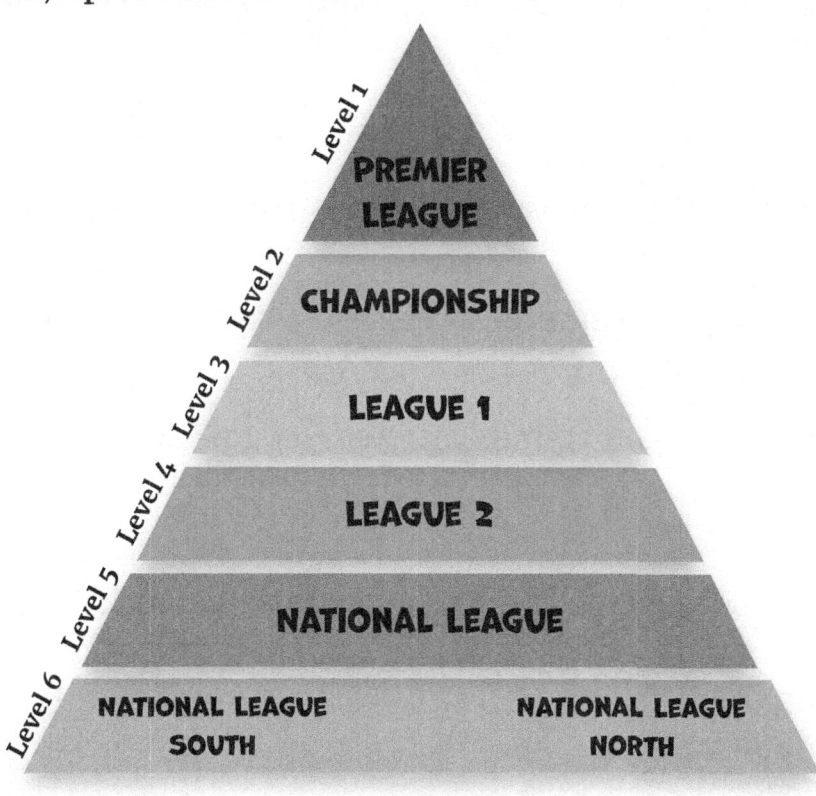

7.5 EUROPE IN A NUTSHELL

Europe runs on two tracks at once: **domestic leagues** at the weekend (the marathon) and **continental cups** in midweek (the spotlight nights). Clubs earn places in next season's continental cups by finishing high enough in their own league (and sometimes by winning their national cup). Many continental formats start with a **group stage** and end with **knockouts**; some rounds are played over **two legs** (home and away), with a one-match **final** at a neutral venue.

Domestic life never stops: league points **at the weekend**, national knockout cup rounds sprinkled in, and those shiny midweek ties where clubs from different countries meet. That's why squads **rotate**—big weeks stack up quickly.

Quick cues (three to remember):

- League places this year usually decide **continental places** next year.

- Midweek **continental**, weekend **league**—same squad, different rhythm.

- Some knockout rounds are **two-legged**; the **final** is one game.

> **FACT:** Many continental cup seasons begin with a **group stage** and finish with **knockout** rounds, so clubs need **squad depth** for a long, two-track campaign.

7.6 INTERNATIONAL MAP

National teams are organised into **six** continental **confederations**: **Africa (CAF)**, **Asia (AFC)**, **Europe (UEFA)**, **North, Central America and the Caribbean (CONCACAF)**, **South America (CONMEBOL)**, and **Oceania (OFC)**. Each runs **regional championships** and the **qualifying** paths toward the global championship held every **four years**. Seasons include **friendlies**, **qualifiers**, and **finals tournaments**; players leave their clubs during **international windows** to represent their countries.

Regional tournaments crown a **continent's champion**; global finals bring the **best teams** from each continent together. **Youth** versions exist too (different age groups), helping young players taste international football early.

Quick cues (three to remember):

- Players switch from **club shirts** to **country shirts** during **international windows**.

- **Qualifiers** lead to regional finals and the **global finals** every four years.

- **Confederations** run their own **tournaments** and **qualifying** formats.

> **FACT:** There are **six** continental confederations in world football, and their **qualifiers** can run for **two to three years** before a global finals tournament.

7.7 INSIDE A FOOTBALL CLUB

A club is like a small **city**: lots of people doing quiet jobs so **eleven** can shine on **matchday**. At the top, **owners** and a **board** choose direction and **budgets**. On the grass, the **head coach/manager** leads training, picks the **team**, and sets the **style**. Around them are **assistant coaches**, a **goalkeeping coach**, **fitness staff**, and **physios** who keep players ready.

Future stars grow in the **academy**—young teams training after school, learning **skills**, **schoolwork**, and good **habits**. **Scouts** travel to watch players live, filing reports on **talent** and **character**. **Analysts** turn matches into **clips** and **numbers**, helping coaches spot **patterns** and **set-piece** ideas. The **media team** tells the club's story—**interviews**, **photos**, **match updates**—while **community staff** run school visits and **fan events**.

Quick cues (three to remember):

- **The board** sets direction; **the coach** sets the team.
- The **academy** grows tomorrow's players.
- **Scouts** and **analysts** help the coach decide **who to sign** and **how to play.**

> **FACT:** **Academy players** combine football with **school education**, and UK academies follow strict rules on **learning time**, **welfare**, and **safeguarding**.

7.8 TRANSFERS & LOANS

Changing clubs is like moving schools: timing, paperwork, and agreement. Most countries have two **transfer windows**—a longer one in **summer** and a shorter one **mid-season**. First, two clubs agree a **fee** (sometimes with **add-ons**). Then the player agrees a contract: length, wages, bonuses. A **medical** checks health and fitness. It becomes **official** only when the league registers the deal—before the deadline.

A **loan** is a temporary move. The player remains **contracted** to the parent club but plays and trains for another team to gain minutes. Some loans include an **option to buy** (the new club can purchase later) or a **recall clause** (the parent club can bring the player back). For young players, loans bridge **academy** football and the speed of **senior** games.

> **FACT:** When a player's contract ends, they can move as a **free agent**—no transfer fee—once **registration** rules and dates are met.

7.9 JOBS iN FOOTBALL

Matchday looks simple on TV, but it runs on many quiet jobs. The **refereeing team** keeps the game fair; **grounds staff** prepare a safe, even **pitch**; the **physio** looks after bodies; the **analyst** turns clips and data into ideas; **commentators** tell the story so fans can follow.

Ref teams include a **referee** in the middle, two **assistant referees** on the lines, and a **fourth official** for **substitutions** and technical areas. Some competitions also use **video assistant referees (VAR)**. Grounds staff mow patterns, check lines, and manage the grass so the ball rolls true. Physios help with **warm-ups**, recovery, and **first-response** care for injuries. Analysts cut key moments, spot **set-piece** details, and brief coaches. Commentators and co-commentators explain tactics and moments so the audience catches the **why**, not just the **what**.

7.10 YOUTH PATHWAYS (REALITY CHECK)

Most journeys start the same way: **grassroots**—school teams or local clubs with friends. Some then join a club **academy**, which adds more training, travel, and school support. A few move on to **scholarships** or **professional contracts**, but many don't—and that's okay. Football has many levels to enjoy for life.

What matters at every step? **School first**, **kindness**, and good **habits**. Academies look for **attitude** as much as skill: listening, teamwork, and **resilience** after setbacks. Releases happen; players change positions; bodies grow at different speeds. Keep learning, keep enjoying, and remember there are lots of roles in the game—**coaching**, **analysis**, **refereeing**—if playing at the very top isn't your path.

CHAPTER 8
MATCHDAY CULTURE

Matchday is more than ninety minutes—it's the buzz on the way, the first glimpse of the **grass**, the **scarf** in the air, and the stories you take home. This chapter is your friendly guide to a smooth, happy day whether you're heading to the ground or watching from the **sofa**

8.1 BEFORE THE MATCH

Tickets & timing

Buy tickets from the club's **official** site or ticket office, and look for **family** sections if you're with kids. Check the **kick-off** time (it **can** change) and aim to arrive **45–60 minutes early** to dodge queues, find your seats, and enjoy the **warm-up**.

Travel & entry

Many stadiums **encourage public transport**; some are **cashless** and have limits on **bag size**. Pick a meeting point in case anyone gets **separated**.

Pack light (quick checklist)

Pack light: **phone (charged)**; **tickets or an e-ticket**; a **small clear bag** (if required); a **light rain jacket** or extra layer; a **bottle of water** (if allowed). For younger ears, simple **ear protection** helps when the crowd **roars**.

8.2 STADIUM LAYOUTS & FAMILY AREAS

A stadium is like a small **town** wrapped around a **pitch**. Outside you'll see signs for **gates** and **turnstiles**; inside there's the **concourse** with **snacks**, **toilets**, and signs pointing to **blocks**, **rows**, and **seats**. **Stewards** (in **hi-vis** jackets) are there to help — ask them anything from '**Which way to Block 124?**' to '**Where's first aid?**'.

Seating & zones. Areas are split into **home** and **away** sections, with **family areas** marked on the map. Many grounds offer **accessible seating** and **lifts**; some also have **sensory rooms** for quieter viewing. You may notice **big screens**, a **public address system** for announcements, and sometimes **safe standing** sections where permitted.

Finding your spot. Keep your **ticket** handy — it lists **block**, **row**, **seat** in that order. Follow the signs: **gate** → **block** → **row** → **seat**.

Good to know. Ask a steward early before queues build. Note the nearest **exit**, **toilets**, and **first-aid** point.

8.3 CHANTS AND GOOD ETIQUETTE

Singing together is part of the **fun**. Learn a simple **chorus**, clap along, and enjoy the **rhythm** of the stand. Keep it **friendly**: celebrate your team without insulting people. If a chant feels **unkind**, give it a miss. Don't block **others' views**, don't throw anything, and follow the **stewards'** guidance. The best noise is **joyful**—not hurtful.

- Join the easy bits: **claps**, simple lines, your **team's name**.

- Stay **respectful**: no swearing at **players**, **fans**, or **officials**.

- Celebrate **safely**: stay in your **space**—**high-five**—don't **shove**.

> **FACT:** Most clubs publish **ground regulations** that ban discriminatory or abusive chanting. Breaking them can mean being asked to **leave**, or even receiving a **ban**.

8.4 MASCOTS & MATCHDAY EXTRAS

Matchday has little shows around the **match**. The club **mascot** (a costumed character) greets fans, leads **chants**, and poses for **photos**. Before **kick-off** you'll see players walk out with child **player escorts** and **flag-bearers**; at **half-time** there may be mini-matches, skills contests, or a **crossbar challenge**. **Ball kids** speed up play by returning the ball quickly. Outside, **fan zones** often have music, games and food.

Good to know. Photos with the **mascot** are usually **pre-match** on the **concourse**. **Half-time** gets busy, so toilet and food queues grow — plan your break. Watch the edges of the pitch: **ball kids** work fast, so keep an eye on rolling balls near the **touchlines**.

> **FACT: Player escorts** (the children who walk out with the teams) are chosen through clubs, schools or lotteries, and clubs follow **safeguarding** rules for their participation.

8.5 WHY KIT COLOURS MATTER

Kits aren't just style—they help everyone tell teams apart in a **split second**. If **colours clash** (especially from a distance or under **floodlights**), passes get messy and decisions slow down. That's why teams have **home**, **away**, and sometimes **third** kits; **referees** and **goalkeepers** also wear different colours, so nobody confuses roles. In youth games, simple **bibs** fix most clashes quickly.

8.6 WATCHING ON TV

A TV match is its own little show. In the **studio**, a **presenter** and **pundits** chat tactics and team news before **kick-off** and at **half-time**. During play, a **commentator** describes the action while a **co-commentator** adds quick 'why it happened' notes—pressing, overlaps, or a clever run. A **touchline reporter** shares updates from near the benches. Behind the scenes, a remote **video assistant referee (VAR)** centre can advise the **on-field referee** on big decisions, and a **replay team** selects angles you see in **slow-motion replays**.

CHAPTER 9
FACTS & TRIVIA VAULT

Welcome to your **snack bar** of football knowledge—**bite-sized** facts, neat quirks, and **'wait... really?'** moments. Use these to **impress** friends, spot **clever plays**, and settle tiny arguments **kindly**.

9.1 WEIRD LAWS & RARE SITUATIONS

Here are classics that often trip people up (in a fun way):

1. **No offside** from a **throw-in, goal kick**, or **corner**.

2. **Back-pass rule:** a **goalkeeper** can't handle a **deliberate** kick from a team-mate's foot. **Headers** or **chests** back are **OK**.

3. A **goalkeeper** also can't handle a team-mate's **throw-in**.

4. You can score **directly** from a **corner** and from a **kick-off**.

5. You **cannot** score directly from an **indirect free-kick** or a **dropped ball**.

6. **Dropped balls** are **uncontested**: the referee returns the ball to **one player** and the others stand back.

7. If the ball **hits the referee**, and a team gains an **advantage** (promising attack, possession changes, or a goal), play **stops** and **restarts** with a **dropped ball**.

8. **Double-touch rule:** the taker of a **free-kick**, **corner**, or **penalty** can't touch the ball again until **someone else** does.

9. **Penalties:** the **goalkeeper** must have at least **one foot on, or in line with,** the goal line at the moment of the kick.

10. Offside **'reset':** if a defender **deliberately plays** the ball (not a **save**), a nearby attacker **may be onside** for the next touch.

11. **Own-goal oddity:** you can't score an own goal **directly** from your **throw-in**; if it flies straight in, it's a **corner** to the other team.

12. **Keeper control:** once a **goalkeeper** releases the ball, they can't handle it again until **another player** touches it; otherwise it's an **indirect free-kick**.

13. **Six-second guidance:** goalkeepers are expected to release the ball within about **six seconds** of controlling it with **their hands** (referees use common sense).

14. A **quick free-kick** is allowed even if a **yellow card** is coming; the referee can **issue the caution** at the next stoppage.

9.2 STADIUM ODDITIES & WEATHER MOMENTS

On TV every **pitch** looks the same. Up close, tiny changes in the **ground** and the **weather** can nudge a match towards **crosses**, **long passes**, or careful **dribbling**. Learn the clues and the game makes even more sense.

Size, slope and surface

Pitches must fit inside set **limits**, so some are a little **longer** or a little **narrower** than others. Many have a gentle **crown** from the **centre** towards the **touchlines** to help rain run off — you won't see it, but the ball will **react**. Surfaces can be **natural grass** or approved **artificial turf** (often called **3G/4G**). Both must be **safe, well-maintained**, and **clearly marked** so lines are easy to see.

What it changes: a slightly **narrower** pitch squeezes wingers and rewards quick **combinations**; a slightly **longer** pitch gives more room for **through-balls** and long runs.

Wind and sun

Wind bends **crosses**, holds **high balls** in the air, or pushes **goal kicks** further than expected. **Corner flags** and floating litter tell you which way the **wind is blowing**. Low **sun** creates long **shadows** and **glare**, which makes judging high balls harder — **goalkeepers** might wear **caps**, shade their eyes, or stand a step **deeper** to see better.

What it changes: set-pieces and long passes need different **power** and **curves**; keepers adjust their **starting spots**.

Rain, mud and water

Light **rain** makes the surface **slick**, so passes **zip** and first touches must be **softer**. Heavy rain slows the ball, causes **skids**, and can leave **puddles** that stop it rolling. If **standing water** appears and the ball won't move properly, play **cannot** continue.

What it changes: quick **one-touch** moves feel great on a damp, smooth surface; in heavy rain teams may play **safer**, higher passes to avoid **puddles**.

Cold, frost and snow

Cold air makes the ball feel **firmer** on the foot. In **snow**, a bright, **high-visibility** ball helps everyone see it, and fresh **lines** may be brushed onto the surface. If the lines can't be kept clear or the surface becomes **unsafe**, the match is **stopped**.

What it changes: players keep passes **tidy** and **low**; **officials** check **visibility** and **surface** more often.

Heat and breaks

On very **hot** days, **referees** can order short **cooling breaks** so players **drink** and **recover**. **Hydration** isn't coaching — it's basic **safety**.

What it changes: **tempo** may slow between bursts; squads **rotate** more to keep energy levels steady.

Ground tech

Modern stadiums use **underground drainage** to move water away quickly and, in some places, **undersoil heating** to stop the pitch freezing. **Floodlights** provide even light for evening **kick-offs** and help the **referee** and **assistant referees** judge close calls.

What it changes: more matches can go ahead in **tricky weather**, and the ball behaves more **predictably** on well-drained, evenly lit surfaces.

Referee decisions and safety

If **lightning** appears, thick **fog** hides the ball, or the surface becomes **unsafe**, the **referee** suspends or abandons the match. **Player** and **fan safety** always comes first.

What it changes: sometimes the **smartest decision** is not to play until conditions **improve**.

> **FACT:** The Laws allow different pitch **lengths** and **widths** within limits, so the same team can feel 'more space' at one ground and 'tighter' at another.

9.3 KIT AND NUMBERS TRIVIA

Shirts and numbers aren't just decoration—they **signal roles**, prevent **clashes**, and help **referees** keep track.

Colours and clashes

Teams must wear clearly **different colours**; **goalkeepers** and **referees** must also wear colours different from both teams. If kits clash, the **away** or **alternate** strip is used. **Undershirts** and **leggings** should match the main **shirt colour** so there's no confusion.

Safety and extras

Shin pads are **compulsory** and covered by **socks**. **Jewellery** isn't allowed. **Tape** on socks should match the **sock colour**. **Head coverings** are allowed if **safe** and **secure**.

Numbers: classic meanings

Early shirt numbers often matched roles on a **1–11** scale (these still help you guess positions today):

- **1**: goalkeeper
- **2**: right-back
- **3**: left-back
- **4–5**: centre-backs or holding midfielders
- **6–8**: central midfielders (box-to-box or holding)
- **7** and **11**: wingers
- **10**: playmaker/attacking midfielder
- **9**: centre-forward

Modern squads can use **higher numbers**, but the classic meanings remain a handy guide.

Armbands and badges

A **captain's armband** shows who speaks to the **referee** at stoppages. **Competition badges** and **manufacturer logos** are controlled by competition rules (no club crests in this book).

Goalkeepers

Goalkeepers wear a **distinct colour** from everyone else. **Gloves** are standard; **long** or **short sleeves** are both fine. Outside the **penalty area**, the goalkeeper is treated like an **outfield player** and **may not handle** the ball.

Seasonal and weather choices

Short or **long sleeves** are both allowed. In **cold** weather, **base layers** keep players warm—still **matching kit colours**. In **bright sun**, a goalkeeper might wear a **cap** to reduce glare.

Smart spotting tips:

A sudden **shirt change** before **kick-off** usually means a **colour clash**. A player **without shin pads** must **leave the field** to correct equipment and can **re-enter** with the referee's permission.

> **FACT:** Numbers don't lock a player's job, but **9**, **10**, and **7/11** still commonly point to **striker**, **playmaker**, and **wingers**.

9.4 NATIONAL TEAM NiCKNAMES

Nicknames make teams easy to spot on TV and in quizzes. They're **informal**, kid-friendly labels (not official titles).

EUROPE

- **England — Three Lions**
- **Wales — The Dragons**
- **Scotland — Tartan Army** *(fans)*
- **Republic of Ireland — the Boys in Green**
- **France — Les Bleus** *('the Blues')*
- **Germany — Die Mannschaft** *('the Team')*
- **Spain — La Roja** *('the Red')*
- **Italy — Gli Azzurri** *('the Blues')*
- **Netherlands — Oranje** *('Orange')*
- **Portugal — A Seleção** *('The Selection')*
- **Belgium — Red Devils**
- **Denmark — Danish Dynamite**
- **Croatia — Vatreni** *('the Fiery Ones')*
- **Switzerland — Nati** *('the national team')*
- **Turkey — Crescent-Stars**

SOUTH AMERICA

- **Brazil — Seleção** or **Canarinha** *('little canary')*
- **Argentina — Albiceleste** *('white and sky blue')*
- **Uruguay — La Celeste** *('sky blue')*
- **Chile — La Roja**
- **Colombia — Los Cafeteros** *('coffee growers')*
- **Peru — La Blanquirroja** *('white and red')*
- **Paraguay — Albirroja**
- **Venezuela — La Vinotinto** *('wine red')*

AFRICA

- **Nigeria — Super Eagles**
- **Ghana — Black Stars**
- **Cameroon — Indomitable Lions**
- **Senegal — Lions of Teranga**
- **Côte d'Ivoire — Les Éléphants** *('the Elephants')*
- **Egypt — Pharaohs**
- **Morocco — Atlas Lions**
- **South Africa — Bafana Bafana** *('the Boys')*
- **Algeria — Desert Foxes**
- **Tunisia — Carthage Eagles**

ASIA AND OCEANIA

- **Japan — Samurai Blue**
- **South Korea — Taeguk Warriors**
- **Iran — Team Melli** *('the national team')*
- **Saudi Arabia — Green Falcons**
- **Australia — Socceroos**
- **New Zealand — All Whites**
- **India — Blue Tigers**
- **Indonesia — Garuda**
- **Vietnam — Golden Star Warriors**
- **Philippines — Azkals** *('street dogs')*

<u>Note</u>: Nicknames can vary by **language** and change over time, but these are widely used and **kid-safe**.

NORTH AND CENTRAL AMERICA

- **Mexico — El Tri** (*'the Tricolour'*)
- **United States — Yanks** or **USMNT** (*initialism for 'US men's national team'*)
- **Canada — Les Rouges** (*'the Reds'*) or **the Reds**
- **Costa Rica — Los Ticos**
- **Jamaica — Reggae Boyz**
- **Honduras — Los Catrachos**
- **Panama — Los Canaleros** (*'the Canal Men'*)

9.5 QUICK QUIZZES

Answer **quickly**. Check the **answer key** on the next page.

Set 1 — Weird Laws Classics

1. **True or false:** You can be offside directly from a throw-in, goal kick or corner.

2. Which restart(s) can go straight in for a goal?
   (a) corner   (b) kick-off   (c) both   (d) neither

3. **True or false:** You can't score directly from an indirect free kick.

4. If the taker taps a free kick to themselves and shoots, the decision is:
   (a) goal (b) retake (c) indirect free kick to the opponents

5. **True or false:** You can't score directly from a dropped ball.

Set 2 — Offside & Involvement

1. A defender deliberately stretches to control a pass, mis-kicks it, and an attacker who was in an offside position collects. Decision?
   (a) offside   **(b) play on**

2. A shot hits the post and rebounds to a team-mate who was in an offside position at the shot. Decision?
   (a) offside   **(b) play on**

3. The pass is played backwards, but the receiver is still nearer the goal line than the ball and the second-last defender at the moment of the pass. Offside?
   (a) yes   **(b) no**

4. An attacker is level with the second-last defender when the pass is made. Offside?
   (a) yes   **(b) no**

5. Offside is judged at the moment:
   (a) the passer kicks/heads it   **(b) the receiver touches it**   **(c) the ball is halfway there**

Set 3 — Goalkeeper & Restarts

1. A goalkeeper releases the ball, then picks it up again before anyone else touches it. Decision?
   (a) play on (b) indirect free kick to attackers (c) retake

2. Six-second guidance means:
   (a) the goalkeeper must release the ball roughly within six seconds
   (b) the ball must be in the air for six seconds
   (c) defenders must retreat six metres

3. A team-mate heads the ball back to the goalkeeper. Can the goalkeeper handle it?
   (a) yes   **(b) no**

4. At a penalty, the goalkeeper must have at least:
   (a) both feet on the line
   (b) one foot on or in line with the goal line
   (c) both feet behind the line

5. A goalkeeper catches a team-mate's throw-in. Decision?
   (a) play on
   (b) indirect free kick to attackers
   (c) retake the throw-in

Set 4 — Stadium & Weather

1. Light rain usually makes passes:
   (a) slower   **(b) zip faster**   **(c) stop dead**

2. Heavy rain leaves puddles and the ball won't roll. Should play continue?
   (a) yes   **(b) no**

3. Corner flags blowing hard towards one goal tell you:
   (a) nothing
   (b) wind direction that can bend crosses
   (c) offside position

4. In snow, officials may use:
   (a) a high-visibility ball and refreshed lines
   (b) smaller goals
   (c) no corners

5. **True or false:** Pitches can be different lengths and widths within limits, so some grounds feel tighter or more spacious.

Set 5 — Kits, Numbers & Officials

1. Why must a goalkeeper's kit be clearly different from both teams' outfield players and the officials?
   (a) style
   (b) TV rules
   (c) to avoid split-second confusion in play

2. A player takes a throw-in that flies untouched straight into their own goal. Restart?
   (a) goal to opponents
   (b) corner to opponents
   (c) retake

3. If kits clash on matchday, the easiest youth fix is usually:
   (a) repaint the lines   (b) training bibs   (c) postpone

4. On the fourth official's board, the colour that shows the player leaving is usually:
   (a) red   (b) green   (c) blue

5. Visible base-layers or tape should:
   (a) be any colour
   (b) match the main kit part they sit next to
   (c) be white only

Set 6 — Live Match Spotter (Apply It!)

1. The ball hits the referee and immediately springs a promising attack for the team that didn't touch it last. Decision?
   (a) play on   (b) dropped ball restart

2. An indirect free kick is swung at goal and goes in untouched by any other player. Decision?

(a) goal   (b) goal kick   (c) retake

1. A powerful goal kick catches a wind gust and curls straight into the kicker's own goal without any other touch. Decision?
   (a) own goal
   (b) corner to opponents
   (c) dropped ball

2. At a penalty, the goalkeeper has both feet in front of the line when the kick is taken and saves. Decision?
   (a) play on
   (b) retake the penalty
   (c) indirect free kick

3. A player's visible base–layer socks don't match the kit colour. Decision?
   (a) ignore it
   (b) the player must correct it or leave to change
   (c) yellow card only

9.6 ANSWER KEY

Set 1	Set 2	Set 3	Set 4
1. False.	1. (b) play on.	1. (b).	1. (b).
2. (c) both.	2. (a) offside.	2. (a).	2. (b) no.
3. True.	3. (a) yes.	3. (a) yes.	3. (b).
4. (c).	4. (b) no.	4. (b).	4. (a).
5. True.	5. (a).	5. (b).	5. True.

Set 5	Set 6
1. (c).	1. (b).
2. (b).	2. (b).
3. (b).	3. (b).
4. (a) red.	4. (b).
5. (b).	5. (b).

CHAPTER 10
QUICK REFERENCE & GLOSSARY

This is your backpack card—the stuff you want at your fingertips during a game, on the sofa, or between school and training. Short, clear, and ready to use.

> Tip: peek here before **kick-off**
> and you'll 'read' a match faster.

10.1 LAWS ON ONE SPREAD

Here's the whole game in a minute — kid-easy, match-ready.

Pitch & Ball

A marked rectangle with touchlines and goal lines, a halfway line and centre circle, and two penalty areas with spots and arcs. Size can vary within limits; surfaces are natural or approved artificial. A goal is **posts, crossbar, and net**; the **whole ball** must cross the **whole line** to score.

Players & Time

Two teams of **eleven** (one being the **goalkeeper**). Youth games may use smaller sides. Standard length is **90 minutes** (two halves) with **added time**; youth lengths vary. There is a **half-time** break in the middle.

Start & Restarts

Kick-off to begin each half and after goals. The **ball is in play** unless it fully leaves the **field of play** or the **referee** stops play. **Throw-in** when it crosses a touchline; **goal kick** if attackers' last touch sends it over the goal line (no goal); **corner** if defenders' last touch does.

Scoring

A goal counts when the **whole ball** fully crosses the goal line between the posts and under the bar — no **hands or arms** by the scorer (except the goalkeeper in their area) and no foul in the **build-up**.

Offside (kid-easy)

Being ahead of the ball isn't a foul by itself. You're only penalised if: (1) you're nearer the opponent's goal line than both the ball and the **second-last defender** at the pass and (2) you become **involved in active play**. No offside from a **throw-in, goal kick,** or **corner**.

Fouls & Cards

Kicks, trips, pushes, holds, **handball** (except the keeper in their area) = **direct free kick**. Cautionable offences (e.g., **reckless** fouls, stopping a promising attack) → **yellow card**. Serious foul play/violent conduct or denying an obvious **goal-scoring** opportunity (DOGSO) → **red card**. Referees may play **advantage** if your team keeps a good attack.

Free Kicks

1. **Direct:** You can **shoot** straight at goal.

2. **Indirect:** Must **touch another player** first (referee keeps an arm raised until the second touch). Opponents **must be 9.15 m** back unless the kick is taken quickly and fairly.

Penalty Kick

Given for a **direct free-kick offence** inside the **penalty area** by the defending team. One **kicker** vs the **goalkeeper**; others stay outside the area/arc until the kick.

Throw-in

Two hands from behind and over the head, both feet **on or behind** the line. You **can't score directly** from a throw-in; if it goes straight into your own goal, it's a **corner** to the opponents.

Goal Kick & Corner

- **Goal kick:** Taken from the goal area; the ball is **in play** when kicked and clearly moves.

- **Corner:** Taken from the nearest corner arc; you **can score directly**.

Goalkeeper Basics

A **goalkeeper** may use their hands only in their own penalty area. They **can't pick up** a deliberate **kick** from a **team-mate** or a **throw-in** from a team-mate (headers/chests are fine). They're expected to **release the ball within about six seconds** of controlling it.

Dropped Ball & Oddities

If play stops for something not a foul (e.g., the ball hits the referee and a team gains an advantage), the referee gives a **dropped ball** to restart; you **can't score directly** from it.

10.2 REFEREE SiGNALS CHEAT SHEET

Learn the **signals** and you'll know the decision before the commentator says it.

Restarts & Direction

- **Throw-in:** The **referee** points along the touchline **towards** the **direction of attack**.

- **Goal kick:** The referee's arm points to the **goal area**.

- **Corner kick:** The referee's arm points to the **corner arc**.

- **Direct free kick:** A **firm point** towards the attacking goal (**no arm held up**).

- **Indirect free kick:** Same point **plus** the **opposite arm held straight up** until the ball **touches another player**.

- **Penalty:** The referee points clearly to the **penalty spot**.

Flow Control

- **Advantage:** Both arms swept forward — **play on** because your team has a **promising attack**.

- **Dropped ball:** The referee holds the ball, indicates the **spot**, and hands it to the correct **team or player**.

Discipline

- **Yellow card:** Card shown at **chest or eye level**; the player's **number recorded**.

- **Red card:** Card held **high**; the player must leave the **field of play**.

- **Caution later:** The referee can let a **quick free kick** happen and show the **yellow card** at the **next stoppage**.

Assistant Referee (AR) Flag

- **Offside:** Flag raised, then angled to show **near**, **centre**, or **far** side.

- **Direction:** For **throw-in, corner**, or **goal kick**, the **flag points the way**.

- **Substitution:** Flag held with **both hands above the head**; the **fourth official** shows the board.

Video Help (where used)

- **VAR check:** The referee points to the **ear** — a **silent check**.

- **On-field review:** The referee **draws a rectangle** (TV screen) and goes to the **monitor**. The **final decision** is the **referee's**.

10.3 FORMATION CRIB SHEET

Shapes are just starting maps. Learn the feel of each one and you'll spot them in seconds — and know where chances might appear.

4-3-3

Feels like width and energy. Wingers stretch the pitch while a single **No. 6** keeps the middle tidy. Attacks often end in crosses and **cut-backs**, with **No. 8s** arriving late. Without the ball, it can look like a **4-1-4-1**. Best when you have quick wide players, a mobile **No. 9**, and a calm holding midfielder.

Risk: space behind adventurous **full-backs**, and too much work for the lone **No. 6**.

Quick ID: three up top, spread wide; **one sitter** in front of the back four.

4-2-3-1

Feels balanced. Two holding mids (a **double pivot**) protect and pass, the **No. 10** finds pockets, and full-backs join when safe. In defence, it often slides into a compact **4-4-2**. Best when you have a clever **No. 10** and tidy passers at the base.

Risk: if the **No. 10** is isolated, the **No. 9** can be starved of service; full-backs can be overloaded if wingers drift inside.

Quick ID: two sit side by side in midfield with a clear **No. 10** ahead.

3-5-2

Feels like a strong spine with flying wings. Three **centre-backs** give security; **wing-backs** own the flanks. One striker checks to link, and the other spins behind. Out of.

possession, it becomes **5-3-2**. Best when you have athletic wing-backs and two strikers who complement each other.

Risk: if wing-backs are pinned back, attacks stall; **switches to the far post** can hurt.

Quick ID: three **centre-backs** and **two strikers**; wing-backs starting high.

4-4-2

Feels simple and compact. Two banks of four shuffle as a unit; the front pair **combine** for **knock-downs** and runs. Attacks lean on wide play and quick combinations between the strikers. Best when wingers work hard and the forwards press together.

Risk: can be **outnumbered in midfield** by a **midfield three**; gaps appear **between the lines** if the block stretches.

Quick ID: two strikers side by side; a **flat four** across midfield.

10.4 GLOSSARY (KID-EASY, GAME-READY)

Advantage — The referee lets play continue after a foul because your team **has a promising attack**.

Aggregate — Total score across two legs (one home, one away).

Back post — The goalpost **furthest** from where the cross is delivered.

Between the lines — Space behind the **opponents'** midfield but in front of their defence.

Block (high/mid/low) — Where a team sets up to **defend** on the pitch.

Body shape — How you stand to see the ball and the pitch; **side-on** helps you play forward.

Box midfield — A four-player square in midfield created by tucking in full-backs or **No. 10s**.

Break a line — Pass or dribble **through** a row of opponents.

Captain's armband — Band worn to show who leads **on-field** communication.

Channel — The lane between the wing and the **centre-back**.

Counter-attack — Fast break right after **winning** the ball.

Counter-press — **Trying** to win the ball back immediately after **losing** it.

Cover shadow — The **passing lane** your body blocks while you press.

Cut-back — A low pass pulled back from near the **byline** to a shooter.

Double pivot — Two holding midfielders **side by side**.

Dropping between centre-backs (CBs) — A midfielder stepping into the back line to help the **build-up**.

Dummy — Letting the ball run past you to a **team-mate** as a disguise.

Far post — The post **furthest** from the ball. (Near post is the closer one.)

False No. 9 — A striker who drops into midfield to create space for runners.

Flick-on — A light header or touch that redirects the ball for a **team-mate**.

Form guide — A team's recent results, often shown as **W/D/L**.

Goal difference (GD) — Goals **scored** minus goals **conceded**.

Half-space — The channel between the centre and the wing — great for **passes** and **shots**.

Heat map — A picture showing where a player or team **spends** the most time on the pitch.

Inverted full-back or winger — Wide player who moves inside **towards** midfield or onto their **stronger foot**.

Key pass — The **final pass** leading to a shot.

Lines (of play) — Rows of **defenders**, **midfielders**, or **forwards**.

Low block — Defending close to your own **penalty area** with compact lines.

Marking (man-to-man/zonal) — Staying with a player **or** guarding a space at set-pieces or in open play.

Offside trap — Defenders step up together so an attacker moves beyond the last defender at the pass.

Overload — Outnumbering defenders in a small zone (for example, **3v2**).

Overlap or underlap — Run **outside** the **ball-carrier** or **inside** between defenders.

Pass map — A diagram showing who **passed to whom** and how often.

Press trigger — A cue to start pressing (bad touch, **back-pass, touchline** pass).

Pressing — Team **pressure** to win the ball back.

Progressive pass or carry — A pass or dribble that meaningfully moves you **towards goal**.

Rest defence — The players you leave **ready behind the ball** while attacking to stop counters.

Screening — A holding midfielder **guarding** the space in front of the back line.

Shape — Your team's **overall positioning** without the ball.

Shot map — A picture of where shots **are** taken and how big the chances **are**.

Switch of play — Move the ball quickly from one wing to the **other**.

Third-man run — Two combine so a third **team-mate** bursts through to receive.

Through-ball — A pass threaded **behind defenders** for a runner.

Touchline — The long **boundary lines** of the pitch.

Goal line — The short **boundary lines** of the pitch.

Transition — The instant **possession** changes from one team to the other.

VAR — Video help for big, game-changing decisions (goals, penalties, straight reds, mistaken identity).

Weak side — The **far side** of the pitch with fewer defenders after a shift.

xG (expected goals) — A number showing how likely a shot **is** to become a goal based on **where** and **how** it is taken.

CLOSING NOTE

Thanks for reading — and for caring about football the smart way.

You now know how to read pitch lines like secret instructions, spot offside at the pass, tell fair contact from a foul, and call the restart before the graphic. Use these skills on the sofa, in the playground, or at the ground. Cheer loud, play kind, and remember our three habits: **look carefully, think clearly, play fairly**.

If you enjoyed this book or it helped a young fan in your life, I'd be truly grateful for a **quick, honest review on Amazon**. Just a sentence or two is perfect — it helps other families find the book and tells me what to improve. (No need for fancy words; say what you liked, or what you'd love more of.)

Thank you for spending your time with these pages.

See you at kick-off!

Printed in Dunstable, United Kingdom